Unlock The Power Of Your Shadow

Transform Your Current Life
Past Lives & Parallel Lives
Embrace Your Powerful Authentic Self

Includes Goddess Archetypes

A Feminine Shadow Work Guide Book

HealHouz
1st Edition 2025

HealHouz

1st Edition 2025

CONTENTS

INTRODUCTION

> *"Know Thyself"*
>
> — SOCRATES

I remember the moment when I first encountered my shadow self. It was a chilly autumn evening, and I found myself sitting in a dimly lit room, surrounded by strangers who had gathered for a spiritual retreat. As the facilitator guided us through a meditation, I suddenly felt a surge of emotions I had long suppressed—anger, fear, and shame. I had no idea where they were coming from. I had not done anything to anyone, heck - I hadn't even spoken to anyone. At that moment, I realized these emotions were coming from some hidden part of myself. I refused to be intimidated by them and made it my mission to find the source of these intrusive emotion bombs. I wanted to find the meaning behind these hidden parts of myself and the source of their power. I knew they were not meant to be ignored or feared, but rather acknowledged and embraced.

As a lifelong seeker of spiritual wisdom and practitioner of the mystical arts, I have always been fascinated by the depths of the human psyche. I have a background education in nursing and explored several different vocations. My inner journey has led me to study various traditions and practices, each offering a unique perspective on the nature of the self. Yet, it was the concept of the shadow—the hidden aspects of our being—that truly captivated me. I am a lover of the unseen and yet present aspects of reality, including those parts of us that hold the secrets of our inner being, those parts that are connected to parts of ourselves that we have yet to uncover and express in the light of the day. I truly appreciate the words of Socrates, "Know Thyself".

In this book, I invite you to embark on a transformative journey of self-discovery and empowerment. "Unlock the Power of Your Shadow" is a guide for women of all ages who are ready to explore the hidden depths of their being and embrace their authentic selves. Through the lens of Hindu goddess archetypes—Kali, Durga, Saraswati, and Lakshmi—we will navigate the complex landscape of the shadow self.

These powerful goddesses offer a rich and nuanced framework for understanding the many faces of the shadow. Kali, the fierce creator and destroyer, teaches us about the transformative power of embracing our darkest emotions. Durga, the warrior goddess, shows us how to find strength in the face of adversity. Saraswati, the goddess of wisdom, guides us toward self-knowledge and understanding. And, Lakshmi, the goddess of abundance, helps us cultivate a sense of worthiness and self-love.

Throughout this book, we will explore the shadow self as a hidden or repressed aspect of the personality that holds the key to profound self-awareness, inner strength, and personal power. We will delve into the multidimensional nature of the shadow, tracing its roots in childhood experiences, past lives, parallel realities, and the holographic nature of existence. By challenging our linear notions of time, we open ourselves up to the possibility of healing and transformation on a deep, soul level.

But this journey is not merely theoretical. "Unlock the Power of Your Shadow" is filled with practical tools, exercises, and prompts designed to help you tangibly engage with your shadow self. From journaling exercises to guided meditations, digital resources, and mindfulness practices, you will find a wealth of support as you navigate this transformative path.

I will do my best to share personal and intimate clips and stories from my life where the shadow has reared its head and brought to my attention its painful existence. Being an aspect of me, that is presenting itself in its powerless state, I can promise you that it won't look pretty or graceful. But instead, raw and unflattering, and quite frankly, it can also be embarrassing. But I feel that it is important to share these with you so that we can normalize bringing peace to the shadow self and extend the hand of cooperation in healing and acknowledging that we are far more powerful and beautiful in our complexity than we realize.

I do understand that everyone's shadow journey is unique and specific to where they are in their journey of life and that there is probably no book that can actually be a true step-by-step guide. Where one person is at in their journey, another will be at a far different place in their destination. But, it is my hope and prayer that in sharing my personal stories and interpretations of their source and purpose, you will find your shadow journey far easier (and hopefully proceed faster) than I have.

At its core, shadow work is about coming home to ourselves—embracing all parts of our being with compassion and understanding. It is about recognizing that our shadows are not something to be feared or avoided, but rather a source of immense power and authenticity. By shining a light on these hidden aspects of ourselves, we can begin to integrate them into our conscious awareness, creating a sense of wholeness and vitality.

If you are ready to unlock the power of your shadow self and step into a life of radical authenticity and fulfillment, this book is for you. Together, we will embark on a journey of self-discovery that will challenge you, inspire you, and ultimately transform you. With the wisdom of the goddesses as our guide, we will explore the depths of our being and emerge stronger, wiser, and more empowered than ever before.

So take a deep breath, open your heart, and let us begin this sacred journey together. Your shadow self is waiting to be acknowledged, embraced, and celebrated. Are you ready to unlock its power?

1
UNDERSTANDING THE SHADOW SELF

Have you ever felt like a part of you lurks just beneath the surface, waiting to be acknowledged? It might happen during a heated argument or when you're all alone, reflecting on your day. That moment when a surge of unexpected emotion catches you off guard, leaving you wondering where it came from. The shadow can also present itself as a nagging fear or regret causing your heart to ache, but not knowing exactly why or where it is coming from. This is the shadow self, whispering truths you might have long ignored. It's a part of us all, hidden yet powerful, and understanding it can lead to profound transformation. One of my early encounters with my shadow came unexpectedly, during a meditative practice where, instead of calm, I found myself overwhelmed by raw, unfiltered emotions. It was as if a mirror had been held up to me, reflecting not just the pretty and likable parts of me, but some past memories of shame and feeling like a fraud. I was angry and felt that I was doing something wrong and deceitful - like I was leading the people around me down a path of inevitable doom. As I followed my emotions, a scene unfolded in my Third Eye awareness, a priestess wearing a brown beaded linen dress with jet-black hair down to her waist, was conducting a ceremony for a particular group of people. They were the "common people" of the society, and it was her job to lead them in a meditation that was more or less a kind of group hypnosis. She did not want to do this, she knew it was a form of taking away their personal and spiritual freedom, but it was also her job to fulfill the wishes of the powerful ruling "Spiritual Elite Leaders" of the society. The experience was both unsettling and enlightening, setting me on a path to explore the shadow with curiosity and compassion. I was left questioning how this priestess was able to conduct such a powerful incantation of those around her, why was she doing something so unethical, who were the rulers that showed and told her how to do this, what was the purpose for it, and most importantly...why was the priestess obligated to carry out this trespass of personal freedom? This chapter is about just that—beginning to understand your own shadow self and the stories it has to tell.

1.1 DEFINING THE SHADOW SELF THROUGH HINDU GODDESS ARCHETYPES

In our quest to understand the shadow self, we turn to the wisdom of the Hindu goddesses. Unlike their Greek counterparts, who often lack spiritual depth, Hindu goddesses embody profound spiritual insights and connections to the divine, offering a rich tapestry through which we can explore our hidden selves. Kali stands as a powerful figure of creation and destruction, embodying the dualities within us all. She teaches us that embracing our darker aspects can lead to rebirth and renewal, much like the cycle of nature itself. Her fierce energy encourages us to confront what we fear, to destroy illusions, and emerge stronger.

Then there is Durga, a symbol of empowerment and protection. She rides into battle with grace and strength, reminding us that within us, lies the power to protect and nurture our inner world. Durga's energy inspires us to set boundaries, to stand firm in our truth, and to courageously face life's challenges. She embodies the idea that true empowerment comes from within, from acknowledging our full range of emotions and experiences.

Saraswati, the goddess of wisdom and learning, invites us to seek knowledge and clarity. Her association with the arts and learning encourages us to explore our inner landscapes with curiosity and openness. Through Saraswati, we learn that understanding our shadow is not about judgment, but about gaining insight and wisdom. Her gentle guidance helps us navigate the complexities of our emotions, urging us to express and articulate our truths.

Lakshmi, the goddess of beauty, happiness, and wealth, brings grace and levity into our lives. She reminds us that life is about celebrating all that is good and bountiful upon Mother Earth. When you have done your work and life is difficult and darkness is all around, she is there to smile upon you and bless you with a joyful life, abundant in beauty and pleasure.

Contrary to the singular focus of Jungian shadow work, which often emphasizes the darker aspects of the psyche, the Hindu goddesses offer a holistic approach. Kali's non-duality, for instance, contrasts sharply with Jung's more linear perspective, highlighting the interconnectedness of all aspects of the self. This broader perspective allows us to see our shadows not just as flaws to be corrected, but as integral parts of our wholeness.

These goddesses also invite us to consider the cultural and spiritual contexts that shape our understanding of the shadow. In Hinduism, spiritual practices such as meditation, chanting, and offerings are intertwined with the worship of these deities, creating a rich environment for exploring the self. Engaging with these practices can provide us with tools to access deeper layers of consciousness, facilitating a more profound integration of the shadow.

As we explore these archetypes, we begin to see how they relate to our personal growth and shadow integration. Kali's fierce love teaches us to embrace our imperfections, while Durga's strength reminds us to protect our inner sanctity. Saraswati encourages us to seek understanding and to learn from our experiences rather than be defined by them. These goddesses, with their diverse attributes, guide us toward a deeper understanding of ourselves, helping us to integrate our shadows and awaken to our true potential.

In connecting with these archetypes, we find a path to self-discovery that is both empowering and illuminating. By embracing the wisdom of Kali, Durga, Lakshmi, and Saraswati, we can transform our shadows from sources of fear and shame into wellsprings of strength and authenticity. It's a path that invites us to live fully, to honor all parts of ourselves, and to step into the light of our true selves. With the guidance of these powerful figures, we embark on a journey of healing and transformation, unlocking the power of our shadows and embracing the fullness of who we are.

1.2 CHILDHOOD ROOTS OF THE SHADOW

Childhood is a time of wonder, innocence, and discovery. However, it is also a period when the seeds of our shadow selves are often sown. The dynamics within our families, the influences of our caregivers, and the early experiences we encounter all play a crucial role in shaping who we become. A child, like a sponge, absorbs everything—words, actions, and even the unspoken telepathic messages from those around us. In this formative stage, we unconsciously begin to hide away parts of ourselves that seem unwelcome or unloved. These hidden parts, tucked away in the shadows, can profoundly impact our adult lives.

Consider a child who grows up in a household where love is conditional upon achievement. In such an environment, the child might learn to suppress feelings of inadequacy or fear of failure to gain approval. These emotions don't just disappear; they retreat into the shadows, manifesting later as a relentless drive for perfection or an underlying fear of rejection. The shadow self, shaped by these early experiences, can lead to behaviors and patterns that seem inexplicable until we trace them back to their origins.

Family dynamics significantly contribute to the formation of the shadow. Parental influence, whether nurturing or neglectful, leaves a lasting imprint. A child who feels ignored might develop a shadow aspect that fears abandonment, leading to adult relationships characterized by clinginess or avoidance. Similarly, a child who witnesses conflict may internalize a shadow trait that avoids confrontation, hindering their ability to assert themselves. These traits, rooted in childhood, persist into adulthood, affecting how we interact with others and perceive ourselves.

Psychological theories offer insights into how childhood experiences shape the shadow self. Attachment theory, pioneered by John Bowlby, suggests that the bonds we form in early life influence our emotional responses and relationships later on in life. Secure attachments foster confidence, while insecure attachments can lead to shadow traits like anxiety or dependency. Social learning theory, developed by Albert Bandura, posits that we learn behaviors by observing others, especially during childhood. If a child witnesses aggression or dishonesty, they may internalize these behaviors, even if they conflict with their conscious values.

To illustrate these concepts, let's consider the story of an individual who grew up in a family where emotions were seldom expressed. As a child, they learned to hide their feelings to maintain peace at home. This suppression became a shadow trait, resulting in an adult who struggles to express emotions openly. Recognizing this pattern allowed them to begin the process of integration, slowly learning to embrace and articulate their emotions without fear of judgment.

Our childhood shadows often manifest in adulthood as fears, insecurities, or patterns we can't quite explain. The fear of rejection, for example, may stem from experiences of neglect or criticism in childhood. As adults, this fear can manifest in self-sabotaging behaviors, such as avoiding risks or seeking constant validation. By understanding the childhood roots of these traits, we can begin the work of integrating our shadows, transforming them from barriers into bridges to self-awareness and growth.

Although I am not a big proponent of blaming everything on what my parents or caretakers did or did not do for me, I can say that I had my share of childhood "issues" to work through. When I was about 3 years old, my mother and I went to visit her parents (my maternal grandmother and grandfather). We were visiting them on the heels of my mother needing a break from the strain of her marriage with my father. Of course, at the time, I only really understood that, "we had left Daddy and that we were going to go visit Grandma and Grandpa". I remember being very quiet, not wanting to say anything for fear that the people around me would come and go and change again. I just figured that if I became quieter, then there would be less for anyone to get angry about. When I got into my teen years, my mother confided in me that, indeed, this had been a terrible time for her. She had a very distant and sad look on her face as she confirmed that there had been a lot of yelling, fighting, violence, and even a gun entering the story at some point. Fortunately, I don't consciously remember all the details. But I know they are somewhere in there, inside of me.

But here is the kicker, my emotions and behavior were so shut down and repressed that my Grandparents concluded that I was "retarded". There was a lot of talk among the adult family members, telling my mom that I needed to be tested for my intellectual ability because "something was wrong with her". I did not interact normally and play with the other children around me. Sometime later, my mother did indeed take me to a woman child psychiatrist to be evaluated.

She asked me questions and let me pick out a jelly bean candy every time I answered one of her questions. When the jelly beans were all gone, she told me she had more of them, if I would like to keep talking to her. The incentive must have worked because I remember eating three little bowls of jelly beans, one by one. And I must have passed the "not being retarded" test because I went on to enter Kindergarten with the rest of the five-year-olds in my class.

This shadow memory reared its head in my early college days, when I would vacillate between feeling like I could never make it through college and at other times feeling like I needed to prove to everyone else that I COULD make it through college. This shadow haunted me my entire first year and one day I just got tired of feeling like I was on a ping pong table and told the universe that it better show me why I am feeling like this or else I am just going to give up college life and go back home. Memories started to filter and bubble up to my conscious mind...I felt so much sadness for the little girl inside of me who was so grief-stricken that she refused to speak out of fear that the one person that was nearest and dearest to her, her mother, would leave her behind. Oh, the pain of childhood!

I was also furious with my grandparents who, in their attempt to make myself and my mother's bad situation of estrangement from my father better, made me their scapegoat by pointing out my flawed and weak character was a sign of some sort of mental deficiency. When in reality, I was successfully navigating a traumatic experience by detaching myself from the pain around me and holding tight to my inner world of glitter rainbows and unicorns. All of this to say, as these memories came flooding back to me, I did my best to reassure my inner little girl that she was ok and that it was the surrounding adults that were "crazy" and that she was far more intelligent than she even realized and very much able to make it through college.

Exploring the shadow requires courage and compassion. It means revisiting those early experiences with a gentle lens, understanding that the traits we developed were ways of coping with a complex world. As we peel back the layers of our past, we gain insight into the shadow's origins, allowing us to reclaim the parts of ourselves that we once deemed unworthy. This process isn't about blaming our caregivers or dwelling on the past; it's about recognizing how our early environment shaped us and choosing to embrace all aspects of our being. Through this understanding, we can begin to forge a path toward healing and wholeness, acknowledging the shadows of our childhood as integral to our journey of self-discovery.

1.3 PAST LIVES AND THE SHADOW

The concept of past lives has always intrigued me, much like a puzzle with pieces scattered across time. Imagine living countless lives, each one leaving an imprint on your soul. These experiences carry lessons, fears, and wisdom that weave into the fabric of who you are today. It's as if the shadow self is a tapestry, threaded with memories and emotions from lives long gone. Some call it karma, the idea that the actions and choices of our past selves echo through time, shaping our present realities. These echoes influence our thoughts, behaviors, and even the unspoken stories we tell ourselves. They manifest as patterns—recurring themes that we can't quite shake off, like a melody playing in the background of our lives.

Past life regression therapy offers a window into these ancient echoes. This therapeutic practice uses hypnosis to access the subconscious, allowing individuals to explore memories and emotions from previous incarnations. By revisiting these past life experiences, one can uncover shadow aspects that have been carried forward into this life. Dolores Cannon was a pioneer in hypnosis and past life regression. She first discovered "past lives" while developing her technique for hypnosis she named and trademarked, the "Quantum Healing

Hypnosis Technique QHHT". Up to this time, past life regression was considered a fringe aspect of the psyche. Dolores formalized its existence in our human consciousness through her scientific and rigorous methods. Imagine sitting comfortably in a quiet room, guided by a therapist's soothing voice. As you relax, your mind begins to wander through the corridors of time, revealing images and emotions that feel both foreign and familiar. You might find yourself reliving moments of joy or trauma, moments that explain certain fears or desires in your current life. The beauty of this therapy lies in its ability to bring understanding and healing. By acknowledging the shadows of past lives, you can release old patterns, freeing yourself from their influence.

The metaphysical basis for past lives extends beyond mere belief. Many spiritual traditions embrace the concept of reincarnation and karma. Karma suggests that our deeds, good or bad, create ripples that extend beyond a single lifetime. These ripples shape the circumstances we encounter, the lessons we must learn, and the shadows we must face. It's a cycle of growth in action and consequence, driving the evolution of the soul. Understanding this concept may help you recognize that the shadows you wrestle with today might be remnants of choices made long ago.

I've witnessed remarkable transformations in individuals who have explored their past life shadows. Take, for instance, the story of a woman who always feared drowning, despite never having a near-drowning experience in her current life. Through past life regression, she discovered a life where she perished at sea. This revelation was both liberating and healing. By confronting this shadow, she was able to release the fear, which had unconsciously dictated her actions. Another individual, struggling with inexplicable guilt, uncovered a past life where she betrayed another person, and it cost them their life. Recognizing this helped her forgive herself, not just for the past, but also for the self-criticism she carried in her present life.

I have personally had past life regression therapy and also see past lives. Seeing past lives is like a movie reel being projected inside of my mind. At first, it might seem disorienting, like you have 2 or more realities going on inside of your mind at once. Actually, you kind of do because this is where the energy of your current personality and that of a past life personality, intersect in your current life. One is being affected by the other, and there is a soul contract with yourself to integrate and heal that past part of yourself with your current personality. Before you were born, your soul predetermined that these 2 lives would intersect at a particular moment when your soul deemed that you are ready to become more than you currently are. You are ready to bring forward and add this dimension of your "past" life self to your current self. When it is presented to you in the shadow form, all hell can break loose.

This is because a past life shadow self will often present itself in a debilitated state. Meaning that the power the personality had in that former life, is currently repressed or debilitated so that it is not able to overpower your current life personality. Conversely, the opposite can be true; if past life personality was disempowered, then the shadow aspect presenting itself in this life can overcompensate and overexaggerate that quality. I have found this to be a common theme with conditions like anxiety or even illness. This is a safety mechanism of sorts so that the current personality does not get overpowered (or overcome) by the past life. By communicating with the past life shadow and asking it to reveal its story to you, you can get a better understanding of how it ended up being stuck where it is (evolution-wise). Past life shadows usually have a traumatic experience attached to them, which creates a "stopping" or "sticking point" for the personality. The current self personality must shine a light towards or cast a light upon the shadow to reveal the suppressed or hidden experience or character trait that needs to be integrated into the current self. By doing so, you transmute what was once a disempowered part of yourself to an empowered part of yourself.

One of my favorite heroines is Dorothy Eady, AKA Umm Sety. Dorothy was born in the United Kingdom in 1904 and, at the age of three, suffered a concussion as a child and was pronounced dead by an attending doctor. As the doctor was telling her parents that she had died, young Dorothy walked into the room, having literally come back from the dead. As she grew up, she had an unexplained connection with the ancient Egyptian artifacts that she saw while visiting a London museum at age four with her parents. She said, "These are my people" and later went on to work in the museum to be closer "to her people". Eventually, she made her way to Abydos, Egypt, and to the *Abydos Temple of Seti* (built by King Seti I (1290-1279 BC). At this time, she called herself Umm Sety, quickly learned hieroglyphics, and remembered her past life as a temple priestess who committed suicide due to falling in love with King Seti I and becoming pregnant with his child. Umm Sety courageously faced her past life shadows as a condemned priestess and powerfully contributed to Egyptian archeology by helping excavate and chronicle the hidden secrets and history of the Abydos Temple of Seti, while also performing the same prayers and rituals in the temple, that she had also held sacred in her previous life.

These stories are not isolated. They illustrate the power of understanding our soul's history in a multi-life format and how it integrates our shadow self. These past life insights don't just explain the shadows; they offer a path to healing and transmutation. By recognizing these shadows as echoes of our soul's journey, we can embrace them with compassion and understanding. This process isn't about living in the past, but about acknowledging it as part of our growth. Each past life is a thread in the grand tapestry of our existence, contributing to the depth and richness of our shadow self.

1.4 PARALLEL LIVES AND HOLOGRAPHIC REALITY

Imagine, for a moment, that each choice you make branches into a new reality—one where every decision creates an alternate path. The concept of parallel lives proposes that we exist in multiple dimensions simultaneously, each version of us experiencing a different set of circumstances. It challenges the western traditional notion of a singular, linear life, suggesting instead a complex web of interconnected existences. In this web, our shadow selves might manifest differently, shaped by the unique experiences of each parallel life. For instance, in one life, you might be an artist, while in another, a scientist. Each path, with its successes and struggles, influences your shadow, creating a complex web of possibilities for who you are. This idea can be both daunting and liberating, offering a broader canvas to explore your shadow self.

The holographic reality principle adds another layer to this understanding. It posits that our three, four, and five dimensional world is a projection from a two-dimensional surface, much like a hologram. In this view, every part of the universe contains the whole, meaning every aspect of our lives carries within it the potential of all possibilities. This principle invites us to consider that our shadows, too, are not isolated or fixed. They are alive and dynamic, reflecting the myriad choices and experiences across our parallel lives. By embracing this perspective, we can begin to see our shadows not as burdens but as multifaceted expressions of our potential.

These concepts intersect intriguingly with modern physics, particularly through quantum entanglement. Quantum entanglement suggests that particles, once connected, remain linked regardless of distance. This connection mirrors the idea of parallel lives, where our choices in one reality can influence another. This also brings up the subject of Quantum Jumping, which is another tool to understand and affect the outcome of different life possibilities. Understanding this can offer a scientific lens through which we can explore the shadow self. It suggests that the emotions, behaviors, and traits we experience may have roots in decisions made in these parallel existences. For instance, a fear that feels ungrounded in your current life might find its origins in a choice made elsewhere. Recognizing this can offer a new dimension to shadow work, one that acknowledges the complexity and interconnectedness of our lives.

With these ideas in mind, you might wonder how to begin exploring your shadow through this lens. One exercise is to reflect on recurring patterns in your life—those themes or emotions that persist despite your efforts to change them. Consider journaling about these patterns, inviting yourself to imagine how they might play out in parallel lives. This exercise requires openness and creativity, challenging you to step beyond the linear narrative of your current existence. Another practice involves meditation or visualization, where you gently guide your mind to explore these alternate realities. Picture yourself making different choices, experiencing different outcomes, and observe how your shadows respond to these different options and find one that resonates with you. I particularly appreciate the work of Dr. Joe Dispenza. His research, retreats, books, and YouTube channel have done so much to offer people an enlightened and multidimensional understanding of how reality is constructed and how to powerfully integrate and navigate its terrain. All of these, and many more, can offer insights into the deep-rooted dynamics at play, allowing you to expand your awareness into the cosmic truths of your soul.

I believe that this is also where the "Law of Attraction and Manifestation" can be a very powerful intersecting factor in the perception of reality. According to Abraham (Esther and Jerry) Hicks, authors of "The Law of Attraction", what you think about is what you create in your life, for better or for worse. Even if you think about what you DON'T want, it will be what you create in your reality because it is what you are thinking about and attracting to you. If you apply this to parallel realities, then maybe it is also important to know what your other parallel selves are putting their focus on and attracting.

I have had phantom parallel reality memories upon waking up from a deep sleep where I have the feeling that I have been deeply involved in some sort of activity in a parallel universe. I may not even be able to put my finger on what I have been doing, but I know that I have been busy doing something because I wake up exhausted. Like I need a nap from running a 5K marathon. This was particularly true during the time of the Harmonic Convergence of 1987. On August 16 - 17, there was a grand conjunction of the perfect alignment of the Sun, Mercury, Venus, and Mars in the sign of Leo. The conjunction was also trined by Jupiter in Aries along with Saturn and Uranus in Sagittarius. Jose Arguelles celebrated this planetary event by coordinating the first global meditation at sacred sites around the world for peace and harmony according to the ancient Mayan Calendar. It became known as the Metaphysical Harmonic Convergence. I remember being exhausted for about 6 months during this time. About 3 months before the August 16th Convergence and about 3 months afterward. The Harmonic Convergence was deeply meaningful to me, although it didn't mean much of anything to anyone else around me, except for a select few in my spiritual circle of friends. But I do know that at some level I was a very active participant in this cosmic event; not only in this dimension but in other parallel realities and dimensions, praying for / calling in and integrating this cosmic alignment.

I grew up learning that the planets and their movements were an integral part of life. My mother drove me to "the big city" two and half hours away from home for my first astrology reading when I was 15 years old. She was an avid student of astrology, which seemed to provide her with the support she needed for her spiritual journey. I still have her astrology folders stuffed with hand-drawn birth and transit "charts". I think about the hours she spent pouring over reference books and contemplating how the planets (Grahas) affect our personality and perception of the world. She seemed to find some spiritual solace in her studies. Receiving guidance from the Cosmos is quicker and easier these days with the masterful efforts of astrologers like Joni Patry, who created the University of Vedic Astrology and the Joni Patry Daily Astrology App.

There is so much to be curious about, how the layers of time and space within the realms of reality, can affect us in our life on Mother Earth. Such exercises and explorations into reality encourage a sense of openness with the Cosmos as you engage with your shadow. They remind us that our shadows are not static; they are alive, evolving with each decision we make. By exploring the concepts of parallel lives and holographic reality, we open ourselves to a broader understanding of who we are. We acknowledge that our shadow selves are not confined to the experiences of a single life but are enriched by the mosaic of all our existences. This perspective can be empowering, offering new ways to embrace and integrate the shadow self. It invites us to see our shadows as allies in our growth, guiding us toward a more authentic expression of our true selves.

1.5 TIME AS AN ILLUSION IN SHADOW WORK

Imagine, for a moment, that time is not the straight line we often perceive it to be. Instead, think of it as a vast, intricate web where each moment exists simultaneously. This metaphysical belief that time is an illusion challenges our conventional understanding and offers intriguing implications for shadow work. The concept of the eternal now posits that past, present, and future are not separate entities but coexist in a continuous now. This perspective invites us to see our shadow selves as not merely products of a distant past or a future yet to come but as ever-present companions shaping our identity and choices.

Time loops, a fascinating concept in this context, suggest that certain patterns and experiences may repeat until we address the underlying issues. Psychologically, time loops can manifest as recurring thoughts or behaviors that seem to trap us in an endless cycle. By recognizing these loops, we gain insight into the unresolved aspects of our shadow selves. Understanding time as an illusion allows us to break free from these cycles, integrating lessons from both past and parallel life experiences. This integration is a profound aspect of personal growth, enabling us to reconcile with parts of ourselves that we may have long ignored or misunderstood.

Incorporating scientific perspectives, we turn to Einstein's theory of relativity, which revolutionized our understanding of time and space. According to relativity, time is not absolute but relative, influenced by factors such as gravity and velocity. This scientific viewpoint aligns with the metaphysical idea of time as an illusion, suggesting that our perception of time is malleable and subjective. By embracing this understanding, we open ourselves to the possibility of accessing past and future selves, allowing for a deeper exploration of our shadow aspects. Dr. Ibrahim Karim, the Egyptian founder of BioGeometry, is a new "Physics of Quality" and explains a modern energy science that successfully unites science with spiritual insight. More information can be found in his books and YouTube channel. I appreciate his ability to explain how metaphysics and reality are multidimensional in a way that unites ancient Egyptian Wisdom Schools with modern psychology of thought and perception. Techniques such as meditation and visualization can facilitate this process, guiding us to connect with different facets of our being across time. The truth is, we are multidimensional beings...we are also spiritual beings having a human experience.

Our purpose in life on Mother Earth is to become more of who we are by incorporating more dimensions of our "selves" into the personality that is you in this lifetime. Having a human body and being able to have the human experience is the most profound opportunity in the universe for gathering and integrating emotions and experiences. The beauty of having a body and physical density as the vehicle for our personality and emotions is that we get to experience them in a world of duality with passion and depth. We get to cry hard and love hard. We get to experience the duality of all emotions, in a body that can not only allow us to feel them but also have experiences to go along with them. This is so amazing and unique. The more parts of your "selves" that you gather and integrate into your present personality, the more you are moving toward the "wholeness" of your soul. There is so much more of your beautiful "selves" to gather and integrate than you ever imagined.

To experience the timeless nature of shadow work, consider trying an exercise that focuses on the concept of the eternal now. Begin by finding a quiet space where you can sit comfortably, free from distractions. Close your eyes and take a few deep breaths, allowing your mind to settle. Visualize yourself standing in a vast, open field, surrounded by a gentle mist. As you stand there, imagine that each breath connects you to every moment of your existence—past, present, and future. Allow images and emotions to arise naturally, without judgment or attachment. Pay attention to any patterns or themes that emerge, as they may offer insights into the shadow aspects that seek integration.

Another exercise involves creating a timeline of your life, not as a linear progression, but as a circle or spiral that represents the interconnectedness of time. On this timeline, identify significant events, emotions, and decisions that have shaped your shadow self. Reflect on how these moments might be linked, not just in a chronological sense, but through the lessons and patterns they represent. This exercise encourages you to view your life as a cohesive whole, where each experience contributes to the rich tapestry of your shadow work.

As we engage with these exercises, we begin to see our shadows as timeless allies, offering wisdom and guidance from across the ages. Recognizing the illusion of time allows us to embrace our shadows with compassion and understanding, integrating their lessons into our present lives. This perspective empowers us to live authentically, free from the constraints of a linear narrative. In doing so, we unlock the potential for profound transformation, creating a life that honors the full spectrum of our existence.

1.6 EMOTIONAL TRIGGERS AS SHADOW DOORWAYS

Emotional triggers are like sudden gusts of wind on an otherwise calm day, catching us off guard, and stirring emotions we thought were buried. They are significant entry points into understanding our shadow selves because they reveal what lies beneath our conscious awareness. These triggers—whether it's a harsh word from a friend, a critical glance from a stranger, or a missed opportunity at work—are not random. They are mirrors reflecting back our hidden fears, insecurities, and unresolved issues. The moment we react intensely to a seemingly minor event, we are being offered a glimpse into our shadow.

Understanding the origins of these emotional triggers is crucial. Often, they are rooted in unresolved issues from our past, particularly from times when our emotional needs were not met. As children, we might not have had the tools to articulate our pain or fear. We may have learned to suppress these feelings, placing them in the shadows of our psyche. When a current situation echoes a past hurt, it can provoke a strong emotional response. Recognizing this connection helps us not only understand the trigger but also the shadow aspect it unveils.

To engage with emotional triggers effectively, we must approach them with curiosity rather than judgment. One powerful strategy is mindfulness, which invites us to observe our reactions without getting swept away by them. By practicing mindfulness, we can create a space between the trigger and our response, allowing us to explore the emotions that arise. For example, when you feel a surge of anger or sadness, pause and take a few deep breaths. Notice where you feel the emotion in your body. Acknowledge its presence without trying to change it. This simple act of awareness can be transformative, offering insights into the shadow aspects that seek attention.

Journaling is another valuable tool for exploring emotional reactions. When a trigger occurs, take the time to write about it. Describe the situation, your emotional response, and any memories or thoughts that surface. Ask yourself questions like, "What does this remind me of?" or "When have I felt this way before?" These prompts can help unravel the layers of your shadow, revealing patterns, and beliefs that may have been hidden. Through journaling, you create a dialogue with your shadow, fostering a deeper understanding of yourself.

Success stories abound of individuals who have used emotional triggers to integrate their shadow selves. Take the case of a woman who always felt intense anxiety whenever she had to speak in public. Through mindfulness and journaling, she discovered that this fear was linked to a childhood experience of ridicule. By acknowledging this shadow aspect, she was able to work through the fear and gain confidence. In another instance, a young lady who frequently felt jealous in relationships traced this emotion back to a time when she felt overlooked by her parents. Understanding this connection allowed her to communicate more openly with her partner, transforming jealousy into trust.

These stories remind us that emotional triggers, while uncomfortable, are opportunities for growth. They guide us to the parts of ourselves that need healing and understanding. By engaging with our triggers mindfully and reflectively, we can integrate our shadows, transforming them from sources of pain into sources of power. This process is not always easy, but it is deeply rewarding. It requires patience, compassion, and a willingness to face the parts of ourselves we've long ignored. Yet, as we do, we pave the way for a more authentic and fulfilling life.

As we close this exploration of emotional triggers, consider them not as obstacles, but as doorways to deeper self-awareness. Each trigger is an invitation to look within, to understand and embrace your shadow self. Through mindfulness, journaling, and reflection, you can turn these moments of discomfort into catalysts for transformation. Embrace the opportunity they offer and step confidently into the light of self-discovery.

2

TOOLS AND PRACTICES FOR SHADOW EXPLORATION

I once sat across from a woman who shared her story of feeling trapped in a cycle of self-doubt and anxiety, emotions she couldn't shake, no matter how hard she tried. She described it as a shadow that loomed over her, always present but never fully seen. This conversation struck a chord with me, as I've journeyed through similar shadows, seeking ways to illuminate these hidden parts of myself. One of the most profound tools I've discovered is meditation—a practice that has been both a refuge and a revelation. Through meditation, I've learned to sit with my shadow, not as an enemy, but as a part of me worth understanding.

Meditation is like an invitation to step into the quiet recesses of your mind, where the shadows often dwell. It offers a space to observe and explore without judgment, allowing you to access deeper layers of your psyche. Vipassana meditation, an ancient practice rooted in Indian traditions, emphasizes self-observation and mindfulness, leading to heightened self-awareness and emotional balance. As you sit in stillness, you begin to notice the subtle movements of your thoughts and emotions, revealing aspects of the shadow that may have been hidden. This practice helps you see your habitual reactions and start to understand the underlying shadow aspects that drive them.

Guided meditation can be particularly effective in focusing on shadow emotions. These meditations often lead you through visualizations that encourage you to meet and acknowledge your shadow self. Imagine sitting comfortably, eyes closed, as a gentle voice guides you to envision a safe space where your shadow can emerge. Here, you might encounter emotions that are difficult to face—anger, sadness, fear. Instead of pushing them away, meditation invites you to hold space for these feelings, to feel them fully, and to understand their origins. This process can be profoundly healing, as it allows you to integrate these shadow aspects rather than letting them control you unconsciously.

Body scan techniques such as Body Scan Meditation (BSM) offer another approach to meditation, helping you identify areas of tension linked to shadow elements. By directing your attention to different parts of your body, you become aware of where you hold stress or discomfort. These sensations often correlate with emotional blockages or repressed feelings. As you breathe into these areas, visualizing tension melting away, you might uncover emotions you've long ignored. This awareness can lead to a release, allowing you to process and integrate these shadow elements physically and emotionally.

To begin exploring your shadow through meditation, find a quiet place where you won't be disturbed. Sit or lie down in a comfortable position and close your eyes. Focus on your breath, noticing each inhale and exhale. As your mind begins to settle, imagine a warm light filling your body, illuminating every corner of your being. When thoughts or emotions arise, acknowledge them without judgment, allowing them to simply be. Whether you use Vipassana, guided meditation, or body scan techniques, the key is consistency and an open heart.

Meditation also plays a crucial role in emotional regulation, helping reduce reactivity and fostering a sense of calm amidst chaos. By regularly meditating or just quieting the "monkey mind", you create a buffer between stimulus and response, giving you the space to choose how you engage with your shadow. This practice not only enhances your relationship with yourself but also improves your interactions with others, as you become more empathetic and understanding. I have seen countless individuals, including myself, transform through meditation. One woman, who struggled with intense anger, found peace through daily meditation, learning to identify and release her rage and embrace compassion.

I personally gravitate to a technique that is a combination of meditation and internal conversation. I go into a relaxed meditative state of gentle awareness of my breathing and surroundings. Quieting my mind so that I can focus on the hum of a refrigerator or air conditioner...just anything that has a low background noise. And then I see if a conversation emerges out of this relaxed state. Sometimes it is a conversation with another person where I am speaking with them about a topic or issue that is stressful. I know then, that I am dealing with some shadow aspect of my personality where I usually want to control them or the situation instead of seeing the other person in their spiritual wholeness and beauty. By acknowledging the other person's wholeness and affirming that they are also a part of God and their soul is guiding them on their life journey, and they are also on their soul's path, then I can release and bless them on their way instead of being critical and judgmental.

Alternatively, if I am speaking to myself, then I know that I am experiencing my shadow as resistance to something. Usually, I am angry or hurt, or acting stubborn about wanting to be "right" about something. My ego tends to like being "right" and my shadow has no problem jumping in and holding me in an obstinate position so that I resist going with the flow, just so that I can be "right". When I can give up being "right" and ease into allowing the situation to be what it is, then my shadow ego can relax, and I can go into a state of allowance and ease up on the resistant stress of the situation. Gradually, I will be able to let go of my need to control the outcome and increase my trust in the Universe to provide solutions and resolutions. Eventually, personal balance is restored.

These stories remind us of the power of meditation in shadow work. It's not about banishing the shadow but embracing it as a part of who we are. Through meditation, we find the courage to face ourselves, uncovering the hidden parts and welcoming them into the light.

2.1 MINDFULNESS PRACTICES TO UNCOVER HIDDEN SHADOWS

Mindfulness is a practice of being fully present—a simple yet profound way to bring awareness to the subconscious shadows that often drive our actions without us realizing it. Imagine walking down a path, each step an opportunity to feel the earth beneath your feet, the air against your skin, and the rhythm of your breath. This is mindful walking, a practice that anchors you to the present moment, gently pulling you away from the distractions of the mind. It allows you to notice the subtle shifts in your mood and thoughts, offering clues to the shadow aspects lurking beneath the surface. As you walk, you might become aware of an unexpected feeling of tension or unease, a sign of something within your shadow that seeks attention. This awareness is the first step in understanding and integrating these hidden parts of yourself.

Incorporating mindfulness into your daily routine doesn't require grand gestures or elaborate rituals. It's about finding presence in the everyday moments and using them to reveal the shadows that often go unnoticed. Take mindful eating, for example. During your next meal, pause to appreciate the colors, textures, and scents of your food. Chew slowly, savoring each bite, and pay attention to how your body responds. You might discover patterns of emotional eating, where you reach for comfort foods, not out of hunger but as a way to soothe stress or sadness. This simple act of mindfulness can uncover emotional patterns tied to your shadow, offering insights into how you cope with life's challenges.

The connection between mindfulness and self-awareness is powerful, especially in shadow work. By observing your thoughts without judgment, you cultivate a kind of inner clarity that is both illuminating and liberating. When you notice a thought or emotion arise, instead of labeling it as good or bad, simply acknowledge its presence. This act of non-judgmental observation creates space for self-reflection and reduces the influence of the shadow on your behavior. Over time, this practice enhances your self-awareness, helping you see the shadow's impact on your life more clearly. You begin to understand the motivations behind your actions, allowing for a more conscious and empowered way of living.

I've encountered many individuals who have transformed their lives through mindfulness, uncovering shadows that had long been hidden. One woman, who found herself frequently overwhelmed by anxiety, began practicing mindful breathing whenever she felt tension rising. By focusing on her breath, she noticed how certain thoughts triggered her anxiety, revealing a shadow aspect connected to past experiences of insecurity. Another person discovered the root of their impatience through mindful listening. By truly hearing others without thinking about their response, they realized how their need for control stemmed from a fear of vulnerability—a shadow trait they had never acknowledged. These stories illustrate the profound shifts that mindfulness can bring about. It's not a quick fix, but a gentle, ongoing practice that invites you to meet your shadow with curiosity and compassion. As you incorporate mindfulness into your life, remember that the goal isn't to eliminate the shadow, but to understand and embrace it as an integral part of who you are.

2.2 JOURNALING PROMPTS FOR SHADOW REVELATION

Journaling has long been a trusted companion for many on the path of self-discovery. It offers a safe space where you can express your thoughts, emotions, and shadow aspects without fear of judgment. The pages become a sanctuary, a place where the deepest parts of your psyche can be explored and understood. Through the practice of stream-of-consciousness writing, you allow your thoughts to flow freely, unedited and raw. This uninhibited expression can often reveal insights into the shadow self that you might not access through structured thought. As you write, you may notice patterns or recurring themes that signify underlying shadow traits waiting to be integrated.

To guide you in your journaling, consider using targeted prompts that encourage introspection and self-exploration. One powerful prompt is to reflect on a recent emotional outburst. Write about the event in detail, describing what happened, how you felt, and any thoughts that arose. Ask yourself what might have triggered such a strong reaction, and whether it connects to past experiences or shadow aspects. Another useful prompt is to explore a recurring dream. Dreams often speak the language of the unconscious, and by delving into their symbolism, you can uncover hidden messages from your shadow self. What emotions do these dreams evoke? What themes seem to repeat? These journaling exercises provide valuable insights, helping you to understand and integrate your shadow.

The therapeutic benefits of journaling are profound. Many find that the act of writing offers emotional release, a way to process complex feelings that might otherwise remain bottled up. As you put pen to paper, you might experience a cathartic sense of clarity, as if the act of writing helps to untangle the knots of your emotions and thoughts. This process not only aids in understanding your shadow but also brings a sense of peace and acceptance. Journaling becomes a dialogue with yourself, a conversation that deepens your self-awareness and fosters healing. Over time, these insights accumulate, allowing you to see the bigger picture of your shadow work journey and how it shapes your growth.

Consider the story of a woman who used journaling to confront her shadow of self-doubt. She began by writing about her feelings of inadequacy, tracing them back to childhood experiences of being compared to her more successful siblings. Through regular journaling, she unraveled the layers of her insecurity, gradually shifting her perspective to recognize her unique strengths. Another individual found healing by exploring the shadows of anger and resentment in her writing. Delving into memories of past hurts, she realized how these emotions were rooted in a fear of vulnerability. By acknowledging this, she was able to cultivate compassion for herself and others, transforming her relationships. These examples illustrate how journaling can illuminate the path to self-understanding and growth.

To make the most of your journaling practice, set aside dedicated time each day or week to write. Create a ritual around it—perhaps a cup of tea, a cozy blanket, and a quiet space where you can focus. Allow yourself the freedom to write without constraints, trusting that the process itself will guide you to what needs to be revealed. Remember, there's no right or wrong way to journal; the key is to be honest and open with yourself. As you continue to write, you'll likely find that your shadow becomes less of a hidden adversary and more of a familiar, albeit complex, part of who you are. Through the pages of your journal, you engage with your shadow, transforming it from a source of fear into a wellspring of wisdom and authenticity.

2.3 DIGITAL TOOLS FOR MODERN SHADOW WORK

In our increasingly digital world, technology has become an ally in personal growth, offering tools that make shadow work more accessible and structured. For many of us, the idea of using apps and online platforms to explore our inner worlds is both exciting and practical. Meditation apps like Headspace offer guided sessions tailored to help you sit with your emotions and explore your shadow self. These apps provide a gentle structure, guiding you through meditations that focus on various aspects of the psyche, allowing you to access deeper layers of awareness. For those who find meditation daunting or struggle to maintain consistency, these digital resources offer a convenient way to integrate meditation into daily life, making it a more sustainable practice.

Journaling apps like Zenfulnote, Shadow Work Journal, and Prompted Journal have also become valuable companions in shadow work. They often come with prompts designed to evoke introspection and encourage you to explore your shadow aspects. Some apps even allow you to track your progress, offering insights into your emotional patterns and growth over time. This digital approach can be liberating, especially for those who prefer typing over writing by hand. With features like reminders, you can establish a regular journaling practice, ensuring that you engage with your shadow self consistently. These apps create a private and secure space where you can express your deepest thoughts and emotions, knowing that your journey is documented and accessible whenever you need to reflect.

Online communities offer another layer of support, connecting you with others who are also engaged in shadow work. These platforms provide a space for discussion, sharing experiences, and offering encouragement. Being part of a community can be incredibly validating, reminding you that you're not alone on this path. Whether through forums, social media groups, or dedicated websites, these communities foster a sense of belonging and offer diverse perspectives on shadow work. Engaging with others can spark new insights, inspire you to try different approaches, and provide a support network that encourages you to continue your exploration.

The benefits of incorporating technology into shadow work are manifold. Firstly, it enhances accessibility, allowing you to engage with practices and resources anytime, anywhere. Whether you're at home, on a lunch break, or traveling, your digital tools are readily available, making it easier to maintain consistency. Secondly, technology can provide a structured framework, guiding you through exercises and practices in a way that feels manageable and less overwhelming. For those who struggle with where to begin or how to proceed, these digital resources offer a roadmap, breaking down the process into achievable steps.

When selecting digital tools for shadow work, it's important to choose those that align with your personal goals and preferences. Consider what you're most comfortable with—whether it's guided meditations, journaling prompts, or community engagement. Look for apps and platforms that resonate with you, offering features that support your unique journey. Reading reviews and exploring free trials can also help you find the right fit, ensuring that the tools you choose will enhance rather than hinder your experience.

The integration of digital tools into shadow work has been transformative for many. Take, for example, the story of a woman who, after years of struggling to connect with her emotions, found clarity and confidence through a meditation app. By committing to daily sessions, she learned to sit with her discomfort, gradually uncovering shadow aspects she had long ignored. Another individual, who felt isolated in their shadow work, found solace in an online community. Sharing experiences and receiving feedback from others helped them feel understood and supported, motivating them to continue their exploration.

2.4 GUIDED VISUALIZATIONS FOR SHADOW INTEGRATION

Guided visualizations offer a unique and powerful way to explore the shadow self, engaging the imagination to safely navigate the depths of our psyche. Imagine visualization as a bridge, connecting your conscious mind with the hidden, often neglected parts of yourself. It provides a space where you can interact with shadow aspects in a controlled and compassionate environment. Visualization techniques allow you to create a mental landscape, a safe haven where your shadow can emerge without fear of judgment or rejection. This mental sanctuary becomes a place of healing, where you can meet your shadow aspects face-to-face and begin the process of integration.

One effective visualization exercise involves imagining a conversation with your inner child—a part of your shadow often linked to early experiences and unmet needs. Begin by finding a comfortable position and closing your eyes. Take a few deep breaths, allowing your body to relax. Picture a peaceful setting, perhaps a garden or a cozy room, where you feel completely safe and at ease. In this space, invite your inner child to join you. Visualize this child as a younger version of yourself, embodying innocence and vulnerability. As you sit together, imagine having a gentle conversation, asking them what they need or how they feel. Listen with an open heart, offering reassurance and compassion. This exercise can reveal profound insights into your shadow, uncovering wounds and desires that influence your present self.

The power of imagination in healing cannot be overstated. Our minds are capable of creating intricate narratives that shape our reality. By using guided visualizations, you can rewrite these narratives, transforming negative or limiting beliefs into empowering stories. Visualization helps you reframe your relationship with the shadow, seeing it not as an adversary but as a source of wisdom and strength. Through imagination, you can explore different aspects of your shadow self, experimenting with new ways of being and interacting. This creative process fosters self-acceptance and encourages growth, allowing you to embrace your shadow as an integral part of your identity.

Consider the story of a woman who struggled with feelings of unworthiness, a shadow aspect that impacted her relationships and self-esteem. Through guided visualizations, she created a mental image of a wise elder and called upon her to be a mentor and offer guidance and support. In her visualizations, she would sit with this elder, receiving messages of love and acceptance. We all have hundreds of Spiritual Mentors who are just waiting for us to call upon them for loving guidance and support. Over time, these sessions transformed her self-perception, helping her recognize her inherent worth and potential.

Another individual used visualization to confront a shadow of fear and insecurity. By imagining and calling upon a protective guardian to keep her safe, she approached her shadow self and was able to speak with this shadow part, coming to understand that the shadow was a past life aspect of herself that had been forced to leave the safety of its tribe. The shadow was a man living alone in a jungle forest who was banished by the tribal elders for breaking a warrior code of conduct. Although he had not taken another person's life, he had caused his tribe "to lose face" and was an embarrassment to his proud group of people. This past life experience caused a fracture point in the soul's personality's development and eventually in this life, her soul called her to come face to face with this shadow. With the help of calling upon a protective guardian guide (whose spirit also happened to be one of the elders of the tribe who had banished the warrior), she was able to face her fear and insecurity with compassion for the ousted warrior and overcome her fear of abandonment.

These stories highlight the transformative potential of guided visualizations. They illustrate how visualization, used to call upon our Spiritual Guides, can lead to significant breakthroughs, offering clarity and healing where it may have seemed elusive. Through the power of guided visualizations, you can create a safe space to explore and integrate your shadow, fostering a sense of wholeness and authenticity. Visualization is a tool that invites you to call upon your Spiritual Guides to help you engage with your shadow in a way that feels safe, nurturing, and empowering, allowing you to step into a fuller understanding of yourself. Embracing this practice can open doors to self-discovery and transformation, helping you unlock the hidden potential within your shadow.

2.5 BUILDING EMOTIONAL RESILIENCE THROUGH SHADOW PRACTICES

Emotional resilience is like a sturdy tree that bends and sways with the wind but remains firmly rooted. It allows us to navigate life's unpredictable challenges with grace and strength. When you engage in consistent shadow work, you're essentially nurturing this resilience. By facing the parts of yourself that are often hidden or denied, you cultivate an inner fortitude that equips you to handle difficult emotions and situations. Shadow work brings to light the fears and insecurities that can leave you feeling vulnerable and confused. But as you work through these shadows, you gradually build resilience, learning to stay grounded even when confronted with emotional triggers that once overwhelmed you.

There are several techniques that can help you stay grounded during these times. One effective method is to practice grounding exercises, such as visualizing roots growing from your feet into the earth, anchoring you firmly. This imagery can be particularly helpful when you're in the midst of a strong emotional reaction, reminding you of your stability and strength. Another technique involves the use of affirmations that reinforce your resilience. Phrases like "I am strong" or "I can handle this" can serve as powerful reminders of your inner capacity to withstand life's storms.

Reflective practices also play a key role in enhancing emotional resilience. By taking the time to reflect on past experiences, both positive and negative, you gain valuable insights into how you've navigated challenges before. This reflection allows you to identify patterns in your behavior and recognize the resilience you've already demonstrated. It can be empowering to see how far you've come, reinforcing your ability to face future challenges with confidence. Consider keeping a resilience journal, where you record instances of personal strength and growth. Over time, this journal becomes a testament to your resilience, a source of inspiration when you need a reminder of your capability.

Emotional resilience has a profound impact on relationships. When you become more resilient, you reduce reactivity, allowing for more thoughtful and compassionate interactions. Instead of reacting impulsively to a partner's comment or a friend's criticism, resilience gives you the space to pause, consider the situation, and respond from a place of understanding. This shift can transform relationships, fostering a deeper connection and mutual respect. I've witnessed firsthand the transformative power of resilience in relationships. One woman I spoke with used shadow work to address her fear of abandonment, a shadow that often led to conflict with her partner.

Through resilience-building practices, she learned to communicate her needs more effectively, creating a stronger bond with her partner based on trust and empathy. She shifted from telling her partner what "you" need to do, to only giving "I" statements. This is an exercise in not using the word "you" when speaking with your partner. You can only use the word "I"... I feel this, I feel that, I would like this, I don't want that...you get the idea. This exercise helps identify the unempowered shadow part that is suffering from the fear of abandonment because when you make a statement and use the accusatory word "you", the shadow can maintain the disempowered state and blame the other person. When you only use the word "I" and only make "I" statements, the shadow must be confronted because "I" statements are, by their very nature, empowered statements. They may come out as raw and ugly statements of one's truth, but at least they are no longer powerless statements of blame upon another person. This is a very powerful first step in transmuting a powerless shadow into a powerful source of authenticity.

Personal growth through resilience is a journey filled with the opportunity for transformation. Another individual found that by cultivating resilience, she was able to break free from the cycle of people-pleasing—a shadow that had dictated her actions for years. People-pleasing is a vicious trap that women (and some men) can find themselves bound and gagged by. The current culture of Patriarchy, by its nature, puts women in a subservient position and one's societal value and self-worth are tied up in being a good servant to others (particularly to men). The subservient wife syndrome comes to mind. It is hard to place the blame squarely on the shoulders of our foremothers for perpetuating this sin since they were most likely indoctrinated and victims of it as well. The question is; do we go back as far as the introduction of patriarchy to our society? If so, this also begs the question of whether or not there was matriarchy before patriarchy. If so, then I presume that there are untold amounts of abuse and neglect that must have taken shape around matriarchy as well. I personally, have had past life memories of the matriarchal society existing in areas where there are now ancient Megalithic female figural structures, like those of Malta, in the Mediterranean Islands. Society was ruled by women and men were useful but not necessary, other than for procreation, work, and recreation. Sometimes, we just need to take an even bigger step back and realize that there may be a much larger picture at play than just this current life.

By looking at people-pleasing from this past life perspective, we can come to understand that possibly we have played both sides, matriarchy, and patriarchy. And it is our purpose this lifetime to find balance with both extremes. This newfound resilience can allow for setting healthy boundaries in both serving and receiving, leading to more authentic and fulfilling relationships.

As we draw this chapter to a close, remember that emotional resilience is not an inherent trait, but a skill that can be developed through practice and dedication. By engaging with your shadow and implementing these techniques, you strengthen your resilience, opening the door to a life of greater stability, understanding, and connection. The journey of shadow work is ongoing, continuously offering opportunities for growth and self-discovery. In the following chapter, we'll explore how to integrate your shadows into daily life, embracing authenticity and empowerment.

3
INTEGRATING SHADOW WITH DAILY LIFE

I once met a woman at a retreat who seemed to have everything—a successful career, a loving family, and a vibrant social life. Yet, she confessed to feeling a profound emptiness, a sense that she was living someone else's life. Her days were filled with obligations and responsibilities, leaving little room for introspection. In her quest for fulfillment, she stumbled upon shadow work. It became her sanctuary, a place where she could explore her true self. But like many of us, she struggled to find time for it amid her busy schedule. This chapter is for those of us who, like her, seek to balance the demands of daily life with the transformative practice of shadow work.

Integrating shadow work into your daily routine begins with intention. Just as you schedule meetings, family activities, or gym sessions, setting aside dedicated time for shadow exploration is crucial. This commitment anchors your practice, ensuring that it doesn't become an afterthought. Consider creating a weekly shadow work schedule, blocking out specific times when you can focus on introspection without interruption. For some, early mornings might be ideal, offering a quiet, reflective start to the day. Others may find solace in the stillness of the evening, using this time to unwind and connect with their inner world. The key is consistency—choosing regular intervals that align with your lifestyle and energy levels.

Daily reflection periods, even if brief, can profoundly impact your journey of self-discovery. Imagine setting aside just 10 minutes each day to journal about your emotions or meditate on a particular shadow aspect. This regular engagement keeps your practice alive, allowing you to delve deeper over time. It also reinforces the idea that shadow work isn't a one-time event but an ongoing process of growth and healing. By making these moments a priority, you honor your commitment to yourself, acknowledging the importance of understanding and integrating your shadow self.

Time management is an art, especially when balancing shadow work with other responsibilities. Practical tools and techniques can help you navigate this challenge effectively. Time-blocking, for example, allows you to allocate specific times for introspection, ensuring that your practice doesn't get lost in the shuffle of daily tasks. By blocking out time for shadow work on your calendar, you treat it as a non-negotiable appointment with yourself, reinforcing its value. Prioritizing tasks is another essential strategy, helping you make room for shadow exploration amid competing demands. Consider creating a to-do list that includes shadow work as a key priority, alongside other responsibilities. This approach encourages you to view shadow work as integral to your well-being, not just an optional activity.

Despite your best intentions, time-related obstacles can arise, often in the form of procrastination or resistance. These challenges are common, but they don't have to derail your practice. Instead, approach them with curiosity and compassion, understanding that they are part of the journey. When procrastination strikes, remind yourself of the benefits of shadow work and the insights it brings. Sometimes, breaking tasks into smaller, manageable steps can help overcome resistance, making the practice feel less daunting. For instance, if journaling feels overwhelming, start with a single sentence or a few minutes of focused breathing. Over time, these small efforts accumulate, building momentum and confidence.

I do want to take a moment and touch upon the difference between procrastination and "processing". Procrastination usually has overtones of self-defeating behavior...in other words, if you just moved forward and did the deed...then you would be better off for it. "Processing" on the other hand, is where your subconscious self is working very hard to come in balance with your personal self and doing the work that your spirit or soul, is calling it to do. In other words, you are working hard on some part of you, but no one else can see it. You might even be physically and/or emotionally exhausted and not even know why. Some cues to know when you are "processing" are; desperately wanting or not wanting to talk to someone else about the topic of your shadow work, feeling like you don't have enough room in your brain to think about another shadow work topic, wanting to take a nap (I recommend that you do), feeling like you need to go do something to distract yourself from what you are thinking about. Everyone has a different way of "processing" their inner shadow work, and it is perfectly ok to take a day or two off, even make a "note to self" saying that you are "processing today". It is a perfectly acceptable way to validate and affirm your shadow work journey.

TIME MANAGEMENT TIPS FOR SHADOW WORK

1. **Set Clear Goals**: Define what you hope to achieve with your shadow work each week.
2. **Establish a Routine**: Consistency is key. Whether it's mornings or evenings, stick to a regular schedule.
3. **Minimize Distractions**: Create a quiet environment, free from interruptions, to enhance focus.
4. **Celebrate Progress**: Acknowledge your dedication and the insights gained along the way.

3.1 CREATING A SUPPORTIVE ENVIRONMENT FOR SHADOW WORK

There's something powerful about stepping into a space that feels uniquely yours, a sanctuary where you can lay bare your soul without fear or distraction. When it comes to shadow work, the environment you create can significantly influence your ability to connect with those deeper parts of yourself. Imagine designating a specific corner of your home as your shadow work haven. This space doesn't need to be elaborate; it just needs to invite you to explore your inner world. A simple chair by the window, a nook with soft lighting, or even a cozy spot in your bedroom can become your sacred space. The key is to choose a place where you feel safe and comfortable, a place that signals to your mind that it's time for introspection.

Setting up a physical space that encourages reflection requires a bit of creativity and personal touch. Start by considering the colors that surround you. Soft, calming hues like blues, greens, or gentle earth tones can soothe the mind and create a sense of tranquility. Lighting also plays a crucial role. Harsh, bright lights can be jarring, while softer, dimmed lights can help ease you into a more meditative state. You might add elements that resonate with you personally, like a favorite piece of art, a decorative scarf or shawl placed over a chair or footstool, a collection of stones or crystals, or a plant that brings life into the room. Incorporating comforting items like cushions, blankets, or a favorite throw, candles, and incense can also enhance the coziness of your space, making it a place you look forward to visiting.

Preparing emotionally for shadow work is just as important as setting up your physical space. Before you begin, take a moment to ground yourself. This might involve practicing deep breathing exercises or a short meditation to center your thoughts. Imagine roots growing from your feet, anchoring you to the earth, providing stability, no matter what emotions arise. This grounding technique can be particularly helpful when you're about to confront challenging aspects of your shadow, offering reassurance that you are supported and secure. As you prepare, it's important to check in with yourself, acknowledging how you feel in the moment. By doing so, you create a safe mental space where you can explore without judgment.

I recall a friend who transformed a cluttered attic into her personal sanctuary for shadow work. Initially, it was a space filled with forgotten items and dust, but she saw its potential. With a bit of effort, she cleared the space, added a comfortable chair, and adorned it with her favorite colors and personal mementos. She even placed a small water fountain, whose gentle trickle became a soothing backdrop for her reflections. This transformation wasn't just about aesthetics; it was about creating a refuge where she felt free to delve into her shadow self. The act of creating this space was, in itself, a part of her shadow work, reflecting her commitment to self-exploration. These days you can find She Shed kits and build your own outdoor She Shed...a grown woman's version of the outside childhood play fort.

Another story comes to mind of a woman who found solace in nature. Her garden became her sacred space, a place where she could sit among the flowers and trees, feeling connected to the earth and her own inner landscape. The natural world provided her with a sense of peace and grounding, making it easier for her to engage with her shadow work. Her surrounding fairy and elemental friends helped her to feel the ebb and flow of her emotions, mirroring the cycles of nature, and offering insights into her own growth and transformation.

Whether indoors or out, the environment you create for shadow work should reflect your personal needs and preferences. It's about finding what resonates with you, what draws you into that deeper connection with yourself. By dedicating a space for introspection, you signal to your subconscious that you are ready and willing to engage with your shadow, fostering an atmosphere of openness and acceptance. This space becomes a sacred container for your journey, holding not just your reflections and insights, but also your hopes and healing.

3.2 SELF-COMPASSIONATE APPROACHES TO SHADOW INTEGRATION

In the delicate process of shadow work, self-compassion stands as a gentle ally, offering a buffer against the harsh voice of the inner critic. This critic—often relentless in its judgment—can impede progress, creating barriers that keep us from fully embracing our shadow selves. Self-compassion, however, nurtures an environment where exploration and healing become possible, allowing for a tender acceptance of all parts of ourselves. Loving-kindness meditation can be a powerful practice in cultivating this compassion. By focusing on thoughts of love and well-being, first for yourself and then extending to others, you invite a sense of warmth and acceptance that can soothe the critical mind. It's as though with each meditative breath, you send waves of kindness through your being, softening the edges of self-doubt and fear.

Affirmations also play a significant role in fostering self-acceptance. Simple phrases like "I am enough," or "I embrace all parts of myself," when repeated with sincerity, can begin to reshape the narrative we hold about our worthiness. These affirmations, spoken or written, act as gentle reminders that imperfections are not flaws to be erased but integral aspects of our human experience. They challenge the critical voices and invite a more compassionate dialogue with ourselves. This practice doesn't demand that we ignore our faults, but rather encourages us to meet them with understanding and patience. Remember, behind every powerless "flaw", hides your own powerful authenticity.

Implementing self-compassion throughout shadow work involves specific strategies that emphasize kindness and understanding. Journaling exercises focused on self-gratitude are particularly effective. Start by writing down three things you appreciate about yourself each day. These could be qualities, small acts of kindness, or moments of resilience. Over time, this exercise shifts your focus from shortcomings to strengths, reinforcing a compassionate relationship with yourself. Another technique is to visualize a nurturing figure or Spirit Guide—someone who embodies unconditional love and support. Imagine what they might say to you or listen for their words of guidance in moments of self-doubt. This visualization can provide comfort and encouragement when you need it most, reminding you that compassion and support from the Universe is always available.

The impact of self-compassion on personal growth is profound. It creates a foundation where progress is not measured by perfection but by a willingness to face oneself honestly. By reducing self-judgment, self-compassion accelerates growth, freeing you from the paralyzing grip of guilt and shame. It allows you to engage with your shadow self from a place of curiosity and openness, rather than fear. This shift in perspective can turn moments of struggle into opportunities for insight and transformation. You begin to see setbacks not as failures but as integral steps in your development.

There are countless stories of individuals who have transformed their lives through the power of self-compassion. A woman I know who constantly battled feelings of inadequacy found solace in loving-kindness meditation. By allowing her mind to dwell on the fact that she was an extension of the Unconditional Love Of The Universe, she was able to silence and bring peace to the little girl of her childhood who was repeatedly told, "She should be more like her older sister". Her older sister excelled in almost everything she did and was seen as nearly perfect by her parents. She, on the other hand, was never good enough. At least, that is what her inner child heard and believed. Over time, this practice helped her silence the critical voice that insisted she was never good enough. By embracing self-compassion, she began to appreciate her unique qualities, which she once overlooked.

These experiences highlight the transformative potential of self-compassion in shadow work. They remind us that true integration of the shadow self is not about eradicating imperfections, but about embracing them with kindness. Once they reveal their source of pain and powerlessness, you can compassionately transmute their pain to personal power. Through practices like loving-kindness meditation, affirmations, and gratitude journaling, we cultivate a nurturing inner environment where all aspects of ourselves are welcome. In this space, we find the freedom to explore our shadows without fear, allowing for profound healing and growth. As you continue your shadow work, let self-compassion be your guide, offering a gentle touch and a warm presence as you navigate the depths of your inner world.

3.3 INCORPORATING SHADOW WORK INTO PROFESSIONAL LIFE

Integrating shadow work into the professional realm can be transformative, not just for individuals but for entire workplaces. Imagine a team where each member possesses heightened emotional intelligence, where empathy flows naturally, and understanding is the norm rather than the exception. Shadow work can lead to such profound changes, as it encourages you to explore and reconcile the hidden aspects of your personality that often surface in professional settings. By engaging with your shadow, you become more aware of your emotional triggers and behaviors, allowing for increased empathy towards colleagues. This awareness fosters a work environment where communication is open, and conflicts are resolved with greater ease. You begin to see your coworkers not as rivals or obstacles, but as fellow travelers on the path of growth, each with their own shadows to explore.

Incorporating shadow work into your workday doesn't require grand gestures or disruptions. Simple, discreet practices can seamlessly fit into your routine, offering benefits without drawing attention. Consider mindful breathing techniques during breaks. A few deep breaths, focusing on the rhythm of your inhale and exhale, can ground you, helping to reset your mind and emotions. This practice creates a moment of pause, allowing you to respond to challenges with clarity rather than react impulsively. Over time, this mindfulness becomes second nature, enhancing your interactions and decision-making processes. Another strategy involves reflecting on daily interactions, perhaps during a quiet lunch or on your commute home. Ask yourself what emotions were triggered during the day and how they relate to your shadow. This reflection fosters self-awareness, guiding you in addressing unresolved issues that might otherwise affect your work.

Leadership plays a crucial role in modeling shadow integration within a professional setting. Leaders who engage with their shadow selves can inspire their teams to do the same, creating a culture of openness and vulnerability. By acknowledging their own imperfections and embracing them with honesty, leaders set the tone for a supportive work environment. They demonstrate that it's acceptable to explore one's shadow, paving the way for others to follow suit. This transparency can transform the workplace, fostering trust and collaboration among colleagues. When leaders engage in shadow work, they become more attuned to the needs and emotions of their team, leading with empathy and understanding.

Consider the story of a company that faced high employee turnover and frequent conflicts among team members. The leadership decided to introduce shadow work practices as part of their professional development program. Employees were encouraged to explore their emotional triggers and engage in reflective practices during work retreats. They were also led into a guided meditation and asked to identify coworkers who irritated or angered them. Once they could visualize the coworker in their meditative space, they were then asked to focus on seeing their coworker with happiness and peace of mind.

Knowing that this would be difficult, they were encouraged to identify the emotions that were triggered and asked to release these emotions one by one. They were to practice this exercise until all of the negative emotions were gone and they could see their once - counterproductive coworker - as a person of peace and productivity. Over time, the atmosphere shifted dramatically. Teams became more cohesive, communication improved, and job satisfaction increased. Employees reported feeling more valued and understood, leading to greater productivity and collaboration. This transformation wasn't just about improved work processes, but about fostering a deeper connection among coworkers, rooted in empathy and self-awareness.

Another case involved an individual who struggled with assertiveness in her role. She realized that her reluctance to speak up stemmed from a shadow of self-doubt, rooted in past experiences of being dismissed. By incorporating shadow work into her daily routine, she began to address this self-doubt, gradually finding her voice. Her newfound confidence led to more effective communication with her team, ultimately enhancing her professional relationships and performance. Her journey inspired others in her workplace to explore their own shadows, creating a ripple effect of growth and change.

These examples highlight the potential of shadow work to transform professional life. By engaging with your shadow, you can enhance emotional intelligence, build empathy, and improve relationships at work. The practices are simple yet profound, encouraging a deeper understanding of yourself and thereby creating new opportunities for success with colleagues. As you integrate these practices, you contribute to a work environment that values authenticity and personal growth, paving the way for a more harmonious and productive workplace.

3.4 BALANCING SHADOW WORK WITH FAMILY DYNAMICS

Shadow work often uncovers layers of ourselves that have been shaped by our family experiences. It's a fascinating intersection where the past meets the present, offering insights that can profoundly improve our interactions with loved ones. Within families, generational patterns often repeat themselves, creating cycles of behavior that may go unnoticed until we bring them to light. Recognizing these patterns is the first step in breaking free from them. For instance, a habit of avoiding conflict might be traced back to a family history of suppressing emotions. By identifying such patterns, you can address them, fostering healthier communication and relationships within your family.

Involving family members in the shadow work process can be incredibly enriching. It opens up avenues for shared growth and understanding, creating a supportive environment where everyone can thrive. One approach is to initiate family discussions about emotional triggers. These conversations can be eye-opening, offering insight into how each member experiences and reacts to different situations. By sharing your own reflections and inviting others to do the same, you help create a level playing field. It's important to approach these discussions with an open mind and a willingness to listen, recognizing that everyone's shadow is unique and worthy of respect. Sometimes this is easier said than done. Within family dynamics, there can be a lot of emotion! Often explosive emotion. It can feel like opening a can of worms, where they immediately start crawling out from the top of the can. If this is your situation, do not be afraid to seek professional counseling for yourself (and possibly other family members). Professional Counselors are trained in family dynamics and can be very helpful in facilitating effective communication and processing family dynamics and their shadows.

Joint mindfulness practices with children can also be a wonderful way to integrate shadow work into family life. Simple activities like mindful breathing or making gratitude lists can help children develop emotional awareness and resilience. These practices allow children to safely recognize and express their feelings, laying the groundwork for a healthy relationship with their shadow selves. Engaging in these activities together strengthens family bonds, allowing you to support each other in moments of vulnerability. It also models the importance of self-reflection and emotional well-being, values that will serve them well throughout their lives.

Of course, integrating shadow work into family dynamics is not without its challenges. Resistance from family members is a common hurdle, particularly if they are unfamiliar with or skeptical of shadow work. Some may fear the vulnerability it requires or worry about confronting uncomfortable truths. To address this resistance, it can be helpful to frame shadow work as a tool for personal and relational growth, emphasizing its potential to enhance understanding and connection. Patience is key—acknowledge their concerns and invite them to explore at their own pace, without pressure or judgment.

I've seen families transform through the integration of shadow work. One family struggled with recurring arguments that seemed to arise from nowhere. Through shadow work, the parents discovered deep-seated fears of abandonment and rejection passed down to them from previous generations. These shadows were inevitably passed down to their teenage children. By each family member addressing these fears openly, and the parents recognizing their unconscious behavior, they were able to break the cycle, leading to more harmonious interactions. Another family found that by practicing mindfulness together, they created a sense of unity and support. Parental emotional outbursts decreased, allowing the children to become more trusting in expressing their emotions, and the parents learned to listen with greater empathy. These experiences highlight the potential for shadow work to not only heal individuals but also strengthen family connections.

Embracing shadow work within the family requires courage and commitment, but the rewards are profound. It invites you to explore the deeper layers of your relationships, uncovering insights that can lead to lasting change. Through open communication, shared practices, and mutual support, families can navigate the complexities of their shadows together, forging bonds that are both resilient and nurturing. In doing so, you create a family dynamic that honors the full spectrum of human experience, embracing both light and shadow with gratitude and grace.

3.5 COMMUNITY BUILDING AND SHARED SHADOW JOURNEYS

Shadow work, by its nature, often feels like a solitary endeavor. Yet, there is immense power in sharing this experience with others. The support of a community can provide encouragement and companionship, turning the path of self-discovery into a shared adventure. Imagine being part of a group where everyone is exploring their inner landscapes, each bringing unique perspectives and insights. An online forum or support group can offer this sense of connection, providing a space to share experiences and seek advice. In these virtual communities, you'll find people at various stages of their shadow work, all eager to support one another. The shared understanding that emerges can be incredibly affirming, helping you feel less isolated in your struggles.

Connecting with others who share an interest in shadow work is easier than you might think. Local workshops, spiritual or support group meet-ups, shadow work study groups, and retreats focused on shadow exploration are excellent opportunities to meet like-minded individuals. These gatherings offer a chance to learn from experts while also engaging with peers who share your passion for personal growth. At these events, you'll likely encounter others who are just as eager to explore the depths of their being, creating a supportive environment for mutual discovery. Don't hesitate to reach out and introduce yourself—many lifelong friendships have begun at such events, united by the shared pursuit of understanding the self.

The benefits of shared shadow journeys extend beyond mere companionship. Engaging in collective shadow work can enhance personal growth and understanding in profound ways. Group meditation sessions, for instance, provide a unique opportunity to experience the power of collective energy. As you sit in silence with others, the collective energy and shared intention amplify insights, offering improved clarity and understanding that might be elusive on your own. This communal aspect of shadow work fosters a sense of belonging, reminding you that you are part of something larger than yourself. It also encourages accountability, as you are more likely to stay committed to your practice when others are counting on you for support in their journey as well.

Consider the story of a group of women who formed a shadow work circle, meeting regularly to meditate and share their reflections. Through their gatherings, they cultivated a space of vulnerability and trust, allowing each member to delve deeper into their shadow selves. Over time, they found that their collective journeys enriched their individual experiences, providing insights and perspectives that might have remained hidden in solitude. The bonds they formed extended beyond their meetings, offering support and friendship in all aspects of their lives. This sense of community became a cornerstone of their personal growth, illustrating the transformative potential of shared shadow work.

As you navigate your shadow work, I encourage you to seek out these communities and connections. Whether online or in person, the support of others can make a significant difference in your journey. By engaging with a community, you open yourself to new perspectives and insights, fostering a deeper understanding of yourself and your shadow. Remember, you are not alone in this exploration—many others are walking this path alongside you, ready to offer support and companionship. As we close this chapter, keep in mind that shadow work, while deeply personal, is also a shared experience that connects us all. In the next chapter, we'll explore how shadow work intertwines with spiritual and personal development, unlocking even more potential for growth and transformation.

MAKE A DIFFERENCE WITH YOUR REVIEW

Your opinion and review matter and you can make a difference in someone's life by sharing your thoughts with other self-help seekers.

Would you like to help someone just like you—curious about how to ***"Unlock The Power Of Your Shadow"*** but unsure where to start?

- It is simple and FREE! Just leave a review on the platform where you purchased your book. Navigate to the book's product page of the online retailer (like Amazon, Barnes & Noble, Kobo, Google Play, Apple/Kindle Book App).
- Log into your account or product page, and locate the "Write a Review" section to share your thoughts and rating about the book; make sure you're logged in with the account that made the purchase to leave a verified review.
- Or you can leave a book review https://healhouz.com/

Most people choose books based on reviews. So, if you received value from this book, I'm asking you to help other Shadow Work self-help seekers by sharing your thoughts and leaving a review. Thank you so much!!!!

4
EMOTIONAL INTELLIGENCE AND SHADOW MASTERY

Imagine this: you're having a seemingly ordinary conversation with a friend or partner, and suddenly, a wave of frustration or anger washes over you. You find yourself reacting strongly, perhaps more so than the situation warrants. This surge of emotion can be a sign that something deeper is at play, a shadow aspect of yourself that's clamoring for attention. In this chapter, we explore the concept of projection, a common shadow phenomenon that can influence our relationships in profound ways.

Projection is an unconscious defense mechanism where we attribute our own unwanted feelings or traits onto others. This often happens without our realization, acting as a mirror that reflects our inner world onto those around us. For instance, you might perceive your partner as overly critical, only to discover that it's your own insecurities fueling this perception. The act of projection provides temporary relief from emotional pain by externalizing it, but it hinders genuine self-awareness and authentic connections. Recognizing projection is the first step toward emotional maturity and healing.

Common signs of projection include frequent blaming or criticism, especially when these reactions seem disproportionate to the situation. You might catch yourself feeling resentment without a clear cause, or notice a pattern of attributing negative traits to others that you struggle with internally. These moments can serve as clues, guiding you to the shadow aspects you may be projecting. When you find yourself frequently annoyed with a friend's perceived arrogance, it might be worth reflecting if there's a part of you that feels insecure about your own self-worth. Recognizing these signs requires honesty and a willingness to look within, acknowledging that the traits we see in others often reflect parts of ourselves that we are unable to see or refuse to acknowledge.

The psychological roots of projection lie in our defense mechanisms, which serve to protect us from confronting painful emotions or aspects of our shadow self. By projecting, we avoid facing these uncomfortable truths, which could have their origins in childhood or past or parallel life experiences. This avoidance becomes a barrier to self-acceptance, preventing us from developing genuine self-awareness. Over time, these repeated projections can lead to misunderstandings and conflicts, particularly in intimate relationships, where the stakes are higher and emotions run deep.

To overcome projection, it's essential to engage in self-reflection and awareness. One practical exercise involves journaling. Start by reflecting on a recent interaction where you felt a strong emotional response. Write down the details of the situation, your feelings, and any judgments you had about the other person. Then, ask yourself: "Could this be a reflection of something within me?" This prompt encourages you to explore your inner world and identify potential projections. By consistently practicing this exercise, you cultivate a deeper understanding of your emotions and the shadow aspects driving them.

Another strategy is to develop self-confidence and establish a clear sense of identity, separate from others. This involves letting go of past issues and setting firm boundaries, allowing you to recognize and accept your shortcomings without projecting them onto those around you. Building self-confidence helps you own your emotions and traits, reducing the need to externalize them through projection. It's about acknowledging your imperfections and embracing them as part of your human experience. Consider the recent "Let Them" movement that became popular when Cassie Philips shared a personal poem, "Just Let Them" and her tattoo, on social media. In Mel Robbins' book, "The Let Them Theory", this premise is taken further and is a wonderful resource and reminder to focus on the things that you can control and stop wasting time and energy on the things that you cannot control.

Healing from projection is a journey that requires revisiting and forgiving past psychic wounds. Whether these wounds originated in childhood or later life experiences, addressing them with compassion and understanding is crucial. As you work through these projections, you pave the way for more authentic connections, both with yourself and others. This process of healing and integration is transformative, allowing you to experience relationships with clarity and empathy, free from the distortions of projection.

REFLECTION EXERCISE: EXPLORING YOUR PROJECTIONS

Step 1: Recall a recent interaction where you felt a strong emotional response. Write about the situation and your feelings.

Step 2: Reflect on any judgments you made about the other person. Could these be reflections of your own traits or insecurities?

Step 3: Consider past experiences that might have contributed to these projections. Did any painful memories come to the surface? Did you feel the hurt of a childhood experience? Did you see any images that were not connected to this present life? Did you have any phantom memories that you cannot explain? If so, how can you address these underlying issues with compassion?

As you delve into this exercise, remember that projection is a natural human tendency. The goal isn't to eliminate it but to become aware of it and use this awareness to foster deeper self-understanding and healthier relationships.

4.1 EMOTIONAL TRIGGERS AS OPPORTUNITIES FOR GROWTH

Emotional triggers often take us by surprise, surfacing in the most unexpected moments. These triggers are like windows to our unresolved conflicts, offering a glimpse into the hidden parts of ourselves that cry out for attention. Instead of viewing them as mere annoyances, consider them valuable insights into your shadow self. Each trigger is a reflection, holding up a mirror to the unresolved emotions or experiences that linger beneath the surface. When a friend's offhand comment stings more than it should or a minor setback at work sends your mood plummeting, these reactions can reveal the unempowered tender spots in your psyche that have yet to heal. Recognizing triggers as opportunities for growth rather than obstacles can transform your approach to personal development.

Identifying your emotional triggers is a crucial step in understanding your shadow. These triggers often manifest as situations that evoke strong, sometimes inexplicable emotional responses. Perhaps it's the feeling of being overlooked in a meeting or the sudden rush of anger when your partner forgets to call. These reactions, seemingly out of proportion to the event, hint at deeper issues waiting to be addressed. They might be linked to past experiences of rejection, abandonment, or unworthiness that you haven't fully processed. By paying attention to these recurring patterns, you can pinpoint the specific triggers that frequently disrupt your emotional equilibrium.

This awareness is the first step in harnessing your triggers for growth.

To explore the origins and meanings of your emotional triggers, consider using mind-mapping techniques. Begin with a central idea—the trigger itself—and branch out with related thoughts, emotions, and past experiences. As you map, you might notice connections between your current reactions and earlier life events. This exercise helps trace the source of your emotional responses, offering clarity and insight into the shadow aspects at play. For instance, a pattern of anger when criticized might lead back to a childhood where criticism was a constant companion. By revealing these links, mind mapping provides a visual representation of your inner world, making it easier to understand and integrate your shadow.

Success stories abound of individuals who have embraced their emotional triggers as pathways to growth. Take the story of Sarah, who often found herself overwhelmed by anxiety at social gatherings. Through reflection, she realized these feelings stemmed from a fear of judgment rooted in her teenage years. By acknowledging this trigger and its origins, Sarah was able to work on building self-confidence and gradually ease her anxiety. Or consider Tammy, who struggled with jealousy in her relationships. By exploring the jealousy's roots, she discovered feelings of inadequacy from a failed past relationship where she felt perpetually compared to others. This awareness allowed her to focus on being in the present and affirming her self-worth, transforming her relationships into spaces of trust and openness.

Each of these stories illustrates the potential for transformation when we view our emotional triggers as guides rather than enemies. They encourage us to turn inward, to listen to the messages our emotions convey, and to address the shadows they reveal. This shift in perspective can redefine how we experience our emotions, turning moments of discomfort into opportunities for profound personal insight and empowerment. It's about seeing every emotional upheaval as a chance to learn and grow, to delve deeper into our understanding of ourselves. As you engage with your triggers, remember that they are not just obstacles to overcome but valuable teachers who can guide you toward greater self-awareness and healing.

4.2 DEVELOPING EMPATHY THROUGH SHADOW WORK

When I first began to explore my own shadow, I realized how much of my understanding of empathy was limited. I thought empathy was simply about being kind and understanding others' feelings. But as I dug deeper into shadow work, I discovered that true empathy involves recognizing the complexities within ourselves—our fears, our desires, and the unacknowledged parts that shape us. When you integrate these shadow aspects, you enhance your ability to empathize not only with yourself but also with others. Empathy becomes a bridge, allowing you to understand both your own experiences and those of the people around you. It's about acknowledging that everyone carries their own shadows and being open to the stories they hold.

Self-empathy is the cornerstone of this process. It's about extending the same kindness and understanding to yourself that you offer to others. Cultivating self-empathy requires patience and practice. It means being gentle with yourself when you uncover parts of your shadow that are difficult to face. This was a difficult one for me to cultivate. I was raised on the old adage, "Pull yourself up by your own bootstraps". Quite frankly, I wasn't raised with a culture of compassion. My value and worth were measured on what I could do and how well I could do it...and please put your emotions to the side! Even in situations where compassion was expected, you weren't to dwell on it too long, just long enough to get the situation resolved, and then it was time to move ahead.

As I step back and take a look at my life, my greatest opportunities to learn compassion and empathy came out of my own suffering. There has been an ironic, (or karmic) theme running through my life where some of the strongest and most critical parts of myself were where I judged others - I developed empathy from suffering the same malady they were suffering. In other words, where I was harsh and critical of others - I got to suffer and experience for myself, the same thing that I was judging in others. For me, this theme centered around physical health.

I was fortunate and blessed with good health in my younger years. I also judged people harshly for their ill health. Honestly, it was more of a matter that I did not understand why people would allow themselves to be sick or have various conditions that seemed to me unnecessary...just "fix it" was my motto. And well, I did not have much empathy for their suffering and I projected my shadow fear of becoming ill and disabled, onto those who were sick, by being critical and judgmental of their illness.

But guess what, since the universe is just and balanced, it also gave me the opportunity to come into balance with myself by giving me my fair dose of illness and disabling conditions to contend with. I got to have all sorts of experiences with mystery illnesses and disabling autoimmune conditions that gave me no other choice but to have compassion for myself and my own suffering. It was like a whole new world opened up to me. My shadow self no longer had to be burdened with judging other people who were sick or limping around... I was too busy simply trying to get my sick self through life and cope with all the things that I had to do to keep going. My shadow was being liberated and transmuting from a place of judgment upon others, to a place of personal compassion and empathy for myself...and most importantly, for others as well.

One way to nurture empathy is through self-compassion practices. These can be as simple as speaking kindly to yourself during moments of self-doubt or taking a moment to acknowledge your feelings without judgment. By fostering self-empathy, you build a foundation that allows you to extend empathy outward, creating more meaningful connections.

To develop empathy within your relationships, consider incorporating active listening exercises into your interactions. This means giving your full attention when someone speaks, without interrupting or planning your response. Instead, focus on understanding their perspective. Reflect back on what you've heard, showing that you value their experience. Another effective exercise involves role-playing scenarios where you explore different perspectives. This can be done alone or with a partner. By stepping into someone else's shoes, even for a moment, you gain insight into their feelings and motivations. These activities not only enhance your empathy but also deepen your understanding of the shadow aspects at play in your relationships. *Seek first to understand, and then be understood.*

4.3 COMMUNICATION SKILLS FOR SHADOW-INFORMED RELATIONSHIPS

Have you ever found yourself in a conversation where the words exchanged seem to miss the mark entirely, causing frustration on both sides? Miscommunication often arises when unacknowledged shadows creep into our dialogue, casting a shadow on our intentions and words. These shadows, shaped by our fears and insecurities, can warp our communication, leading to misunderstandings and conflict. For instance, if you carry a shadow of inadequacy, you might hear criticism in a partner's casual remark, even if none was intended. This misinterpretation can spiral into defensiveness and arguments, blocking the genuine connection. Recognizing how these shadows influence communication is the first step toward clarity and understanding.

To communicate more effectively, it's helpful to employ strategies that acknowledge and address these shadow influences. Assertive communication techniques can be invaluable in this process. They encourage you to express your needs and boundaries clearly and respectfully, without aggression or passivity. For example, instead of saying, "You never listen to me," an assertive approach might be, "I feel unheard when I share my thoughts, and it's important to me to feel understood." This subtle shift in language opens space for dialogue rather than confrontation, reducing the likelihood of defensive reactions. Nonviolent communication (AKA Adult - Adult Communication) further supports this approach by fostering empathy and connection. It involves expressing your feelings and needs honestly while remaining open to others' perspectives. When you practice nonviolent communication, you create an environment where each person's experiences are validated, paving the way for mutual understanding.

Transparent communication, where honesty and openness are prioritized, can prevent many of the misunderstandings that shadow influences cause. By being forthright about your feelings and shadow aspects, you invite others to do the same. This openness can transform relationships, building trust and deepening connections. Imagine a scenario where two friends have drifted apart due to unspoken resentments. By each acknowledging their shadows—perhaps one feels envy over the other's success, while the other harbors guilt for not being more supportive—they can address these feelings directly. This dialogue not only clears the air but strengthens their bond, demonstrating the power of transparency in healing and reinforcing relationships.

Consider the example of a couple struggling with communication breakdowns. One partner feels neglected, interpreting the other's long work hours as a lack of interest in the relationship. The other, carrying a shadow of fear about financial insecurity, believes they're providing for the future. By recognizing these shadow elements, they begin to communicate more openly. The first partner expresses their need for quality time, while the other shares their financial concerns. This honest exchange allows them to find common ground, demonstrating how shadow-informed communication can resolve misunderstandings and foster closeness.

Another scenario involves a workplace setting, where a team leader notices tension among team members. By introducing shadow-informed communication practices, the leader encourages each member to share their challenges and insecurities. This openness reveals that the tension stems from misinterpreted intentions and unvoiced concerns. As the team members engage in transparent dialogue, they begin to understand each other's perspectives, leading to improved collaboration and morale. These examples illustrate the profound impact of shadow-informed communication on personal and professional relationships. By embracing these techniques, you can navigate the shadows that cloud your interactions, creating a space where genuine understanding and connection thrive.

4.4 EMOTIONAL REGULATION AND SHADOW AWARENESS

Emotional regulation is not just about keeping your cool under pressure. It's about understanding the ebb and flow of your emotions, especially those linked to your shadow self. This part of you holds the emotions and traits that you might have repressed or ignored over time. By becoming aware of these shadow aspects, you gain the power to regulate your emotional responses more effectively. Imagine recognizing a sudden wave of irritation as a sign of an unmet need or an unresolved issue. Instead of reacting impulsively, you pause, allowing yourself to process the emotion without being overtaken by it. This awareness is a skill that can transform the way you interact with the world, providing a deeper sense of emotional stability and balance.

To enhance your emotional regulation and maintain this equilibrium, practical techniques can be your allies. Breathing exercises are a simple yet powerful tool. When you feel an emotional outburst coming on, take a moment to focus on your breath. Inhale deeply through your nose, hold for a few seconds, and then exhale slowly through your mouth. This act of deep breathing can calm your nervous system, helping you regain control over your emotions. It's a way to anchor yourself in the present, giving you the space to choose how you respond rather than reacting out of habit. Similarly, mindfulness meditation can increase your emotional awareness. By dedicating a few minutes each day to sit in stillness and observe your thoughts without judgment, you cultivate a greater understanding of your emotional landscape. You learn to recognize patterns and triggers, creating a buffer between stimulus and response.

Self-awareness is the keystone of effective emotional regulation. It requires you to be attuned to your inner world, acknowledging the emotions as they arise without immediately acting upon them. This awareness allows you to identify which emotions are linked to your shadow and why they surface in particular situations. It involves a willingness to explore these emotions, to question their origins and the beliefs that underpin them. By doing so, you create a foundation for emotional balance, where you are no longer at the mercy of your feelings but rather in partnership with them. This level of self-awareness demands honesty and courage, yet it offers the reward of greater emotional freedom and resilience.

Many individuals have found that shadow work significantly improves their capacity for emotional regulation. Take, for instance, a woman named Lisa, who struggled with anger management.

Through exploring her shadow, she discovered that her anger often stemmed from a deep-seated fear of being unappreciated. By acknowledging this fear and working to address it, she found that her emotional outbursts decreased in frequency and intensity. Another example is a lady named Tamika, who battled with chronic anxiety. By asking her shadow, why are you so fearful and anxious, she realized that her anxiety was connected to feelings of inadequacy that dated back to her childhood. With this insight, Tamika began practicing mindfulness meditation, which helped her remain present and calm even in challenging situations.

4.5 BUILDING AUTHENTIC CONNECTIONS THROUGH SHADOW INTEGRATION

Authenticity in relationships is a bit like the sun breaking through clouds after a storm. It brings warmth and clarity, illuminating the path to deeper, more genuine connections. When you integrate your shadow, you embrace both your strengths and vulnerabilities, allowing you to show up as your true self. This authenticity fosters trust and respect, creating an environment where both you and others feel safe to be open and honest. When you are authentic, you communicate your needs and desires without fear of judgment or rejection, knowing that vulnerability is not a weakness but a bridge to understanding and intimacy with your inner being and others.

The impact of authenticity with yourself and in relationships cannot be overstated. Authentic connections with yourself and others are the bedrock of trust, allowing you to engage with yourself and others on a deeper level. When you are authentic, you invite others to do the same, creating a space where mutual respect thrives. This respect is not just about acknowledging each other's strengths, but about honoring the courage it takes to reveal one's true self. In such relationships, misunderstandings diminish, replaced by empathy and support. You begin to see each other not as perfect beings but as whole individuals, with shadows and light intricately blended together.

To develop authenticity in your relationships, consider engaging in exercises that encourage vulnerability. Find a safe setting where you can practice opening up, perhaps with a trusted friend or partner. Share something personal, something you might usually keep hidden. Notice how it feels to be vulnerable, how the act of sharing shifts your connection with the other person. This exercise is not about oversharing, but about choosing to reveal what is most true to you. As you practice, you build the muscle of vulnerability, making it easier to bring your authentic self into all your interactions.

I remember the story of a woman named Claire, who struggled with showing her true self in her friendships. She feared that revealing her insecurities would lead to judgment or abandonment. Through shadow work, Claire began to embrace her vulnerabilities, understanding that they were part of her authentic self. She practiced opening up to her closest friends and sharing her fears and dreams. To her surprise, instead of judgment, she was met with understanding and support. Her willingness to be vulnerable deepened her friendships, creating bonds rooted in truth and empathy. Another example is Linda, who carried a shadow of perfectionism. By acknowledging this shadow and sharing her struggles with her partner, she found relief in the acceptance of her imperfections. This not only strengthened their relationship but also inspired her partner to share their own vulnerabilities.

Authenticity is one of the most important themes in my life. I have many past life and parallel life shadows around the subject of authenticity. For me, it is like a loaded cannon. There is a lot of emotional and intellectual ammunition loaded in this one. I can recall specific lifetimes being persecuted for my "truth" and authenticity. One is being a "man of knowledge" in the early 1500s, which is a person who has a formal education of higher thinking like philosophy or astronomy, and being disemboweled and tied to a tree and left to die after being labeled a heretic. Another is being a male healer/warlock/doer of the "magical arts" where I was attacked for practicing magic. Society around me was adopting a new rational thought called "logic and medicine". Eventually, I was caught and dropped into a large boiling cauldron of animal fat and essentially cooked alive.

I also have past life memories of "The Burning Times". In 1990, I watched a Canadian documentary called *The Burning Times*, it was about the witch hunts that took place across Europe just a few hundred years ago. Although the documentary is less than an hour long, it felt like an eternity watching it. I became enraged and very emotional. I was so angry that I was crying. When the documentary was over, I felt stabbed in the gut and bludgeoned. It seemed as though all of my powerless shadows came jumping up at me, screaming for attention. It was a profound moment to realize how much I had compromised my truth and authenticity out of fear of social persecution and death. Unfortunately, I cannot give you a nice story about how I wrapped up this shadow and tied it into a bow. I am still dealing with this shadow, but every day I get stronger and stronger. I can promise you one thing, I will not ignore her (my shadow) and I will do my best to listen to the stories she has to tell. I know she is only there to show me the fragmented parts of myself that I need to sew back together again.

When you integrate and transmute your shadow, you grow stronger and pave the way for genuine connections that go beyond surface-level interactions. You create relationships where both you and others can grow and thrive, supported by a foundation of trust and respect. This integration of shadow and self brings a new depth to your interactions, allowing you to experience the richness and complexity of human connection. As you continue to embrace your authentic self, you open the door to a world where relationships are not just about coexistence but about true communion.

In this chapter, we've explored how shadow integration enhances emotional intelligence and relationship dynamics, fostering connections that are as authentic as they are fulfilling. As you embrace your shadow, you step into a fuller version of yourself, inviting others to do the same. This journey of authenticity is a continuous process, one that enriches your life and the lives of those around you. In the next chapter, we will delve into the spiritual and personal development aspects of shadow work, exploring how this integration can lead to a more enlightened and empowered existence.

5
SPIRITUAL AND PERSONAL DEVELOPMENT THROUGH SHADOW WORK

Imagine, for a moment, a small child within you, eyes wide with wonder and a heart full of untapped potential. This inner child is a part of you, carrying the echoes of past experiences, joys, and wounds that shape your present self. Shadow work often involves reconnecting with this inner child, acknowledging their presence, and offering them the love and understanding they might have missed. It's a crucial step in healing, allowing you to integrate parts of yourself that were once hidden away out of fear or necessity. This process isn't just about revisiting the past; it's about reclaiming the innocence and creativity that define your essence.

5.1 THE ROLE OF THE INNER CHILD IN SHADOW HEALING

In the realm of shadow work, the inner child represents a gateway to understanding some of our deepest wounds and most profound truths. It's as if this child holds the key to a hidden garden within, one where forgotten dreams and stifled emotions reside. By reconnecting with your inner child, you embark on a journey to heal past hurts and nurture your authentic self. Visualization exercises can be particularly powerful in this process. Picture yourself in a safe, comforting space—a sun-drenched meadow or a cozy room filled with warmth. Invite your inner child to join you there, to sit beside you and share their thoughts and feelings. This visualization creates a bridge, allowing you to engage in a dialogue with this younger version of yourself, to ask questions, and to listen with compassion.

As you connect with your inner child, you'll likely encounter unresolved childhood wounds that have lingered into adulthood. These might manifest as feelings of abandonment, rejection, or neglect—echoes of moments when your needs went unmet. Recognizing these wounds is the first step toward healing. For instance, the fear of abandonment might stem from a time when you felt unseen by your caregivers. By acknowledging this, you can begin to understand how it influences your current relationships and behaviors. It's important to approach these wounds with kindness, seeing them not as weaknesses but as parts of your story that deserve attention and care.

Healing the inner child involves more than just recognition; it requires nurturing and integration. Creative expression can be a powerful tool in this healing process. Activities like drawing, painting, or storytelling allow you to give voice to your inner child's experiences, and to express emotions that words alone might struggle to convey. Through artistic endeavors, you create a safe space for your inner child to explore and heal. This process is not about achieving perfection, but about allowing your creativity to flow freely, embracing whatever emerges as a reflection of your inner world.

Consider the story of a woman who, through shadow work, discovered her inner child's love of storytelling. As a child, she had often been silenced, her vivid imagination dismissed as frivolous. Reconnecting with her inner child, she began writing stories again, weaving tales that spoke to her deepest truths. Through this creative exploration, she found healing, reclaiming a part of herself that had been lost. Another individual, struggling with feelings of inadequacy, used drawing to reconnect with their inner child. By sketching scenes from their childhood, they were able to process emotions they had long suppressed, gaining insight and acceptance.

REFLECTION EXERCISE: DIALOGUE WITH YOUR INNER CHILD

Find a quiet place where you can sit comfortably, free from distractions. Close your eyes and take a few deep breaths, allowing your body to relax. Visualize yourself in a safe, comforting space—a meadow, a beach, or a cozy room. Invite your inner child to join you there. Imagine this child sitting beside you, open and curious. In your mind, begin a conversation. Ask them how they feel and what they need. Listen to their responses with compassion and understanding. When you're ready, gently open your eyes and reflect on the experience in a journal. Consider what insights emerged and how you might nurture your inner child moving forward.

5.2 GODDESS ARCHETYPES & SPIRITUAL PRACTICES THAT COMPLEMENT SHADOW WORK

Imagine waking up each day with a feeling of peace and purpose, feeling connected to something greater than yourself. Spiritual practices can be the bridge that links your inner world with the broader universe, enriching your shadow work in profound ways. Practices like yoga, meditation, astral travel, vagus nerve reset, chanting, prayer beads, past life regression, dream analysis, tuning fork therapy, Ayahuasca journeys, mindfulness, and many more, create an elaborate weaving of experiences that ground you in the present, while simultaneously illuminating the shadows that linger within. Kundalini yoga, for instance, is a powerful practice that awakens dormant energies, helping you access deeper parts of your consciousness. This form of yoga involves dynamic breathing techniques, movement, and chanting, all designed to cleanse and energize the body and mind. As you move through the postures, you may find yourself releasing emotional blockages, allowing your shadow self to emerge and be embraced.

Mindful movement practices, such as tai chi or walking meditation, offer another pathway to connect body and mind. These gentle, flowing movements encourage you to tune into the sensations of your body, fostering a heightened awareness of the present moment. In this state of mindfulness, you become more attuned to the subtle cues of your shadow self, gaining insights into patterns that may have previously gone unnoticed. By integrating these practices into your routine, you create a holistic approach to shadow work, one that honors both the physical and spiritual aspects of your being.

The synergy between spirituality and shadow work lies in their shared goal of deepening self-understanding. Spiritual practices invite you to connect with yourself on a soul level, encouraging you to confront your fears, desires, and truths with a connection to the cosmos and an open heart. This exploration is not about escaping reality, but about embracing it more fully with clarity and compassion. As you engage in these practices, you may find that the barriers between your conscious and unconscious selves begin to dissolve, revealing the interconnectedness of all aspects and dimensions of your being. This realization can lead to profound spiritual growth, as you come to understand that your shadow is not an adversary, but a valuable teacher on your path.

To support your journey, consider incorporating chakra balancing exercises into your routine. Chakras are energy centers within the body, and when they are out of balance, they can contribute to emotional and physical distress. By focusing on these centers through visualization and breathwork, you can realign your energy, promoting harmony and healing. Imagine a ball of light at the base of your spine, slowly rising through each chakra as you inhale, bathing each one in warmth and light. As you exhale, visualize any negativity or tension being released, leaving you feeling balanced and centered.

Breathwork techniques can also be instrumental in emotional release, offering a direct line to the shadow's depths. Techniques like alternate nostril breathing help calm the nervous system, creating a sense of equilibrium and allowing you to process emotions with greater ease. By dedicating just a few minutes each day to focused breathing, you create a space where the shadow can be accessed and acknowledged without fear.

Consider the story of a woman who found solace in these practices. Struggling with anxiety and self-doubt, she turned to Kundalini yoga as a way to quiet her mind. Through consistent practice, she began to access parts of herself that had been hidden, uncovering a strength and resilience she never knew she possessed. Her spiritual awakening was not a sudden epiphany, but a gradual unfolding, like peeling away the layers of an onion that revealed her true self. Another individual, overwhelmed by stress, discovered the power of breath work and emotional release massage therapy to facilitate pent-up emotions. By focusing on her breath and releasing stress in her muscles and body, she learned to navigate her shadow with grace and compassion, transforming her relationship with herself and the world around her.

These stories remind us of the transformative potential that lies at the intersection of spirituality and shadow work. By embracing the practices that work best for you, you invite a deeper connection with yourself, one that honors the complexity and beauty of your shadow. Through this integration, you cultivate a sense of wholeness and peace, creating the life you have always dreamed of manifesting.

5.3 GODDESS KALI - UNDERSTANDING NON-DUALITY

Kali, the fierce Goddess of time and change, stands as a powerful symbol of non-duality, embodying the paradox of creation and destruction. Her image is both terrifying and beautiful, a reminder that life's contrasts are not to be feared but embraced. In Hindu mythology, Kali emerges during times of chaos, her dance a force that both annihilates and renews. This duality reflects the nature of existence itself—where every ending is a new beginning, and every shadow contains the seed of light. Through Kali, she shows us that our darkest moments are intertwined with our brightest and that true understanding comes from accepting human complexities. Her stories invite us to consider that what we often reject or fear holds the potential for profound transformation.

Embracing non-duality means recognizing that our light and shadow selves are part of a unified whole, not opposing forces. It challenges the binary thinking that categorizes emotions and experiences as either good or bad. Instead, it asks us to see them as complementary, each enriching the other. When you accept both your strengths and your vulnerabilities, you create a space where true healing and transformation can occur. This acceptance is not passive but active, requiring courage to sit with discomfort and uncertainty. You might practice this by observing your thoughts and emotions without judgment, acknowledging their presence, and allowing them to coexist. This practice cultivates inner harmony, reducing the internal conflict that arises from trying to deny or suppress parts of yourself.

The transformative power of non-duality lies in its ability to foster profound inner peace and acceptance. By letting go of rigid labels and embracing the fluidity of your complexity, you free yourself from the constraints of self-imposed limitations. This liberation allows you to live more authentically, guided by a sense of wholeness rather than fragmentation. Consider the story of a woman who found herself caught in cycles of self-doubt and perfectionism, two sides of the same coin. Through exploring Kali's teachings, she began to see her perceived failures not as shortcomings but as natural and integral to her growth. Embracing both her achievements and her mistakes, she discovered a newfound sense of freedom, allowing her to pursue her passions with confidence and joy.

Another example is a lady who struggled with anger, often seeing it as a negative force to be extinguished. By engaging with the concept of non-duality, she learned to view her anger as a signal, a call to action that could be channeled into positive life-changing impetus for growth. This shift in perspective transformed her relationship with herself and others, fostering deeper empathy for her rage and understanding that it is a natural part of human existence. Such stories illustrate how embracing non-duality can lead to personal transformation, inviting you to see yourself and the world around you through a lens of compassion and balance. It's about finding the courage to dance with Kali in both creation and destruction, knowing that each step brings you closer to the heart of your true self.

As you explore Goddess Kali's archetype, as the creator and destroyer of life, you may find that her lessons resonate deeply, offering guidance on how to navigate the complexities of your own life. Her presence invites you to confront the fears and judgments that keep you from embracing your full potential. By recognizing that all aspects of your being are interconnected, you open the door to deeper self-awareness and growth. Kali's dance becomes a metaphor for your own journey, a reminder that every experience, whether joyous or painful, is an opportunity for transformation. In respectful prayers to her, you are encouraged to embrace the richness of your existence, trusting her to show you that in the fusion of light and shadow, you will find the path to wholeness.

5.4 GODDESS LAKSHMI - FOSTERING ABUNDANCE

Imagine a life where abundance flows effortlessly, where you feel supported and prosperous in every aspect. The Goddess Lakshmi embodies abundance and prosperity. Her presence is both nurturing and empowering, guiding you to shift from a mindset of scarcity to one of abundance. This transformation begins by recognizing the areas in your life that feel limited or lacking. It can be as simple as feeling there's never enough time or resources. Goddess Lakshmi invites you to reframe these perceptions, to see the potential for growth and fulfillment in every situation. Prayerful engagement with her energy can be a powerful catalyst for change, helping you embrace a life where abundance is not just a dream but a reality.

Rituals honoring Goddess Lakshmi can be a profound way to invoke her energy and attract abundance. These rituals are not just about material wealth but encompass all forms of prosperity—health, happiness, love, and wisdom. One simple ritual involves creating an altar dedicated to Lakshmi, adorned with symbols of abundance such as coins, flowers, and candles. As you light the candles, focus on what abundance means to you, visualizing your desires manifesting in your life. Another practice is meditative reflection, where you spend a few moments each day seeing and feeling what it is like to live in abundance, asking for Lakshmi's guidance in removing obstacles and opening pathways to prosperity. These rituals imbued with intention and gratitude, align your energy with her blessing of incoming riches and abundance, allowing it to flow into your life.

Overcoming a lack or scarcity mindset requires more than desire; it involves identifying and transforming the limiting beliefs that hold you back. These beliefs can stem from past experiences or societal conditioning, whispering that there is never enough to go around. To counteract this, begin by acknowledging these thoughts without judgment. Write them down, and then challenge their validity. Replace them with affirmations that reinforce abundance and prosperity, such as "The Universe is overflowing with wealth, and it flows to me", "I am surrounded with abundance" or "Prosperity flows to me easily and effortlessly." These affirmations, repeated daily, will gradually reshape your mindset, creating a fertile ground for abundance to flourish.

Integrating an abundance mindset into shadow work complements the process of embracing all aspects of yourself. When you recognize that abundance is your birthright, you can face your shadow with confidence and compassion. This shift in perspective allows you to see the hidden gifts within your shadow, understanding that even your fears of scarcity and doubts of deserving, hold the potential for growth and transformation. By cultivating an abundant mindset, you open yourself to new possibilities, seeing challenges not as obstacles but as opportunities for expansion.

Consider the story of a woman who felt trapped in a cycle of financial struggle. Despite her efforts, she always seemed to fall short (*more month than money*), her dreams of abundance remaining just out of reach. Through prayer to Lakshmi and rituals and affirmations, she began to shift her mindset, focusing on gratitude and possibility rather than lack. Slowly, she noticed changes—unexpected opportunities, supportive relationships, and a newfound sense of confidence. Her life transformed, reflecting the abundance she had embraced within. Another individual, plagued by self-doubt, prayed to Lakshmi for guidance to cultivate self-worth and prosperity. By seeing herself as deserving of abundance, she unlocked doors to success and fulfillment, realizing that her limits were just shadows that had hidden inner gold and riches.

These stories highlight the transformative power of invoking the Goddess Lakshmi. By embracing her principles, you can move beyond scarcity, opening your heart and life to the richness that surrounds you. It's about recognizing that abundance comes in many forms, each enhancing your journey toward wholeness and joy. As you integrate these practices, you will find that abundance is not something you chase, but something you invite.

5.5 GODDESS SARASWATI - A SOURCE OF WISDOM

Consider the quiet moments when clarity feels elusive. The mind, a whirlwind of thoughts, leaves you gasping for air. In these moments, the Goddess Saraswati's wisdom is a beacon of light. Known as the goddess of knowledge and art, Saraswati embodies clarity. She represents the flow of wisdom and insight, the whisper guiding us through the labyrinth of our shadow selves. Connecting with Goddess Saraswati involves inviting her presence into your spiritual practice, using meditation as a conduit. Picture yourself sitting in a serene space, eyes closed, as you visualize a gentle river of light flowing through you. This light carries knowledge, slowly dissolving confusion and illuminating the shadows within. It's a simple yet profound technique that can help you access deeper parts of yourself, allowing insights to emerge naturally.

Goddess Saraswati's teachings encourage a deeper exploration of your shadow aspects, urging you to look beyond the surface. Her wisdom is not about accumulating facts or knowledge but understanding the essence of who you are. To gain insight into your shadow requires a willingness to question and reflect. Consider the patterns that repeat in your life, the emotions that seem to linger without resolution. Saraswati invites you to examine these with curiosity. Are they themes being carried on, over and over again, from past lives? What do they reveal about your hidden fears and desires? What shadows are lurking around, just waiting to be seen in the light of day? By seeking her guidance, she will show you how these patterns are not set in place as obstacles but as opportunities for growth and transformational power.

Applying Saraswati's lessons in daily life involves more than meditation; it requires active engagement with your inner world. One effective exercise is journaling, an act of translating thoughts and emotions into words. Begin by setting aside time to write about a recent experience that challenged or unsettled you. Use prompts like, "What did this experience teach me about my shadow?" or "How can I apply this understanding to my life?" This practice helps Goddess Saraswati transform vague notions into concrete insights, helping you integrate her wisdom into your everyday existence. As you write, allow Goddess Saraswati's energy to guide you, and ask her to bring clarity and understanding to your shadow reflections.

Stories of those who have connected with Saraswati's wisdom illuminate the profound transformations that are possible. Take the example of a woman who felt trapped by indecision, her mind constantly second-guessing every choice. Through meditation and journaling, she prayed for the blessing of Saraswati, asking for guidance in understanding her hesitations. Over time, she realized her indecision stemmed from a fear of failure rooted in her shadow. Recognizing this allowed her to release the fear, gain confidence in her decisions, and embrace the power that had been locked within. Another individual found clarity in the chaos of a busy life by turning to Saraswati. Through daily meditation, where she saw herself sitting at the feet of the Goddess Saraswati, she received peace of mind, learned to trust her intuition, and navigated her life with assurance.

These narratives remind us of the power of Saraswati's insights in shadow integration. Her wisdom is a gentle yet transformative force, inviting you to explore the depths of your being with an open heart. By embracing her teachings, you cultivate a deeper understanding of yourself, illuminating the shadows and revealing the gifts they hold.

Saraswati's presence encourages you to trust your inner wisdom, to see beyond the veils of confusion, and to live with clarity and purpose.

5.6 GODDESS DURGA - STRENGTH IN CONFRONTING SHADOWS

In the richness of Hindu tradition, Durga stands as a formidable warrioress goddess, a beacon of strength and courage. Her image, often depicted with multiple arms wielding weapons, is not just a symbol of power, but a reminder of the resilience we all possess. Durga's presence invites us to confront our shadows with the same tenacity and fearlessness she embodies. When facing the parts of ourselves that we often hide away—those challenging shadow aspects that whisper insecurities and doubts—calling upon Durga's protection and strength can be transformative. Imagine yourself, in moments of doubt, praying to Goddess Durga and envisioning her at your side, her unwavering gaze reflecting your inner power. This visualization reminds you that you are not alone, that within you lies a well of strength waiting to be tapped.

Facing your shadows requires more than just courage; it demands a willingness to embrace what you fear. Often, these are the aspects of ourselves that we've been taught to avoid or suppress—anger, shame, jealousy, fear of inadequacy. Yet, by confronting these shadows, you allow for true growth and understanding. Start by acknowledging what you resist, and naming the emotions or traits you tend to hide. Then, while praying for Durga's strength and being open to her support, lean into them. Sit with these feelings, observe them without judgment, and ask what they have to teach you. This process can be challenging, but it's also empowering, offering insights that lead to profound transformation.

Building mental and emotional resilience is crucial in this process. It's about developing the inner resources to face your shadows repeatedly, each time gaining more clarity and strength. Techniques such as grounding exercises and mindfulness can help anchor you in the present, providing stability as you explore your inner world. Consider practices like mindful breathing or progressive muscle relaxation to reduce tension and promote calmness. By cultivating resilience, you create a foundation from which you can confront your shadows without being overwhelmed.

Empowerment through the Goddess Durga is not just about overcoming fears; it's about reclaiming your power and self-confidence. When you embody Durga's energy, you begin to see yourself as capable and strong, ready to face any challenge that arises. This empowerment is transformative, allowing you to approach life with a newfound sense of confidence. It shifts your perspective, helping you see obstacles as opportunities to grow rather than insurmountable barriers.

There are countless stories of individuals who have been blessed by her and harnessed Durga's strength to integrate their shadows and transform their lives. One woman I met shared how she had long struggled with self-doubt, a shadow that whispered she was never good enough. By asking Durga to bless her life, she began to confront these doubts head-on, questioning their validity and seeking out their roots. Over time, she found the courage to pursue her passions, eventually launching a successful career that aligned with her true self. Another person spoke of her battle with anger, a shadow that often led to conflict and regret. Through meditation and visualization, he connected with Durga, learning to channel her anger into constructive action. This shift not only improved relationships but also empowered her to become an advocate for change in her community.

These stories highlight the profound impact of praying for and embracing Durga's strength. They remind us that by confronting our shadows with courage and resilience, we can transform our lives, stepping into the fullness of who we are meant to be. Durga's presence is a powerful ally in this process, offering the support, protection, and strength needed to face even the most daunting aspects of ourselves. As you continue your journey of shadow work, remember that within you lies the strength of a warrioress, ready to conquer whatever challenges come your way.

6

OVERCOMING CHALLENGES IN SHADOW WORK

Imagine standing at the edge of a vast, unfamiliar forest. The trees are dense, their branches casting mysterious shadows on the path before you. This forest represents your shadow self, a realm filled with both fear and promise. As you step forward, a sense of trepidation may creep in, whispering doubts and uncertainties. This fear, deeply rooted in our psyche, often stems from past experiences and the anxiety of uncovering repressed memories. The mind with its ego, in its quest for survival, can trigger responses akin to fight, flight, or freeze, especially when faced with the unknown aspects of our being.

The roots of fear in shadow work often dig deep into our past. You might recall moments from childhood when emotions were dismissed or belittled, leaving scars that have since woven themselves into the fabric of your shadow. These painful memories linger, manifesting as fear whenever you approach the edges of your conscious awareness. It's the fear of confronting these emotions, of opening doors to past traumas that your mind has long kept locked away. This fear is natural; it's a protective instinct that signals the potential for growth and healing. Yet, fear also holds the key to profound transformation if only you dare to face it.

Understanding that fear is a natural part of the shadow work process is crucial. It signals that you are on the brink of significant personal growth. Embracing this fear, rather than resisting it, can be transformative. Acknowledge it as a companion on your journey, a guide that points to the areas of your soul that require healing and attention. Normalizing this fear allows you to approach shadow work with compassion and patience, recognizing that it's part of the human experience. It's important to remember that everyone who embarks on this path encounters fear; it's not a sign of weakness but of courage.

Managing fear with kindness and self-compassion is essential. Grounding exercises can be particularly helpful during moments of fear. Picture yourself as a sturdy tree, with roots extending deep into the earth, providing stability and strength. During times of heightened anxiety, take a moment to breathe deeply and visualize these roots anchoring you to the ground, offering support and reassurance. This imagery can help you stay present, allowing you to explore your shadow with safety and grounding. Another effective technique is to create a mental safe space, a personal sanctuary where you can retreat whenever fear arises. Imagine a place where you feel completely at ease, surrounded by warmth and comfort. This visualization can serve as a refuge, a reminder that you are protected as you delve into the depths of your shadow.

Consider the story of Maya, a woman who faced her fear of the shadow with remarkable courage. For years, Maya avoided confronting her emotions, fearing the flood of memories that might surface. But when she finally turned inward, armed with the support of a compassionate therapist, she discovered a reservoir of strength she never knew she had. Through meditation and grounding exercises, Maya gradually faced her fears, each step revealing new layers of her shadow. Her journey was not without challenges, yet each moment of fear brought with it a profound sense of liberation. Maya emerged with a deeper understanding of herself, empowered by the very fears that once held her back.

Another example is Emma, who struggled with anxiety rooted in past rejection and judgment. Through shadow work, she realized that her fear was not an enemy but a messenger, highlighting areas of her life that needed healing. By embracing this fear and practicing visualization techniques, Emma developed a newfound sense of resilience. She learned to approach her shadow not with trepidation, but with curiosity and compassion. Each encounter with fear became an opportunity for growth, transforming her perspective and leading to a more authentic, empowered self.

REFLECTION EXERCISE: EMBRACING YOUR FEAR

Take a moment to sit quietly and reflect on a fear that often arises during your shadow work. Close your eyes and breathe deeply, allowing your mind to settle. Visualize a safe space where you feel completely secure. Invite your fear into this space, greeting it with compassion. Ask it what it wants to tell you, and listen closely. Write down any insights or emotions that arise. This exercise is not about eliminating fear but understanding it, allowing you to move forward with greater awareness and strength.

6.1 MANAGING OVERWHELM IN EMOTIONAL EXPLORATION

The weight of emotional exploration can sometimes feel like a tidal wave, crashing over and leaving you breathless. Recognizing when you're overwhelmed is crucial. It's not just about feeling stressed; it's the physical signs that manifest in your body, like fatigue that lingers despite a good night's sleep, or headaches that throb persistently.

These symptoms are your body's way of signaling that it's time to pause and recalibrate. Emotionally, you might notice increased irritability, a tendency to snap at loved ones over minor issues, or a desire to withdraw from social interactions. This withdrawal isn't just physical; it's a retreat into oneself, a sign that your emotional reserves are running low. It's in these moments that the shadow work can feel daunting as if the very act of introspection is a burden rather than a release.

Pacing is your ally in the realm of emotional exploration. Think of it as setting a rhythm for your shadow work, one that honors both your need for introspection and your capacity for emotional resilience. Start by setting realistic goals that align with your current emotional state. If you're new to shadow work, perhaps begin with a single, manageable aspect of your shadow self. Allow yourself the grace to take things slowly, understanding that healing is not a race but a gradual unfolding. Break the work into smaller, more digestible pieces, giving yourself permission to step back when needed. This approach not only prevents overwhelm but also allows for deeper, more meaningful engagement with your shadow. Remember, the goal is not to rush toward enlightenment but to gently peel back the layers of your psyche, one layer (or lifetime) at a time.

Establishing boundaries is vital in maintaining your emotional well-being during shadow work. This means creating clear limits around your exploration, both in time and intensity. Consider setting a timer for your sessions, allowing yourself a fixed period to engage deeply before stepping back into the world. This time-limited approach prevents you from becoming lost in the depths of your emotions, providing a structured way to explore without becoming trapped in an alternate shadow world. Additionally, employing safe words or signals can be incredibly beneficial. These can be agreed upon with a therapist or simply used as a mental cue for yourself, indicating when a particular exploration becomes too intense. This practice not only respects your emotional boundaries but also empowers you to take control of your shadow work process.

Amidst these explorations, stress reduction practices serve as a lifeline, offering moments of calm and clarity. Breathing exercises are a simple yet effective tool to release tension and recenter your mind. Imagine taking a deep breath in, holding it for a moment, and then slowly exhaling, visualizing the stress leaving your body with each breath. This rhythmic breathing can be practiced anywhere—whether you're sitting at your desk, standing in line, or lying in bed—allowing you to ground yourself in the present moment. Incorporating this practice into your daily routine can create a sense of stability, providing a refuge from the emotional storm that shadow work can sometimes stir up.

To illustrate, let's consider the experience of a woman named Lanie. She often found herself overwhelmed when diving into her shadow, experiencing physical symptoms like tension headaches, short temper, and emotional withdrawal. By recognizing these signs and implementing pacing strategies, Lanie was able to engage more effectively with her shadow work. She began setting aside specific times each week for exploration, allowing herself breaks when needed. This structured approach, combined with a daily walk outside in the fresh air, helped her manage the emotional intensity, turning what was once an overwhelming process into a fulfilling journey of self-discovery.

Lanie's story underscores the importance of listening to your body and honoring your emotional capacity. By recognizing the signs of overwhelm and employing these strategies, you can navigate the intricate landscape of your shadow work with resilience and grace, allowing for a more profound and sustainable exploration of your inner selves.

6.2 HANDLING RESISTANCE AND STAGNATION

Resistance in shadow work is like an invisible wall, often appearing when you least expect it. It can manifest as procrastination, where you find yourself avoiding the very activities that could lead to personal growth. This avoidance might look like putting off journaling, skipping meditation, or simply doing all the other tasks that you need to get done, except engaging with your shadow self. It's a tricky dance of knowing what you need to do but feeling an inexplicable pull to do anything else. Then there's self-sabotage, a more insidious form of resistance. It's when you set goals only to undermine them, perhaps through negative self-talk or not following through on commitments. These behaviors can leave you feeling stuck as if you're moving in circles rather than progressing.

To understand why resistance and stagnation occur, it's helpful to delve into their psychological roots. Often, the fear of change looms large. Change, even when positive, can be daunting. It disrupts the familiar, pushing you out of your comfort zone into uncharted territory. This fear can trigger an unconscious desire to cling to familiar patterns, even if they no longer serve you. Maybe you simply fear the unknown. If you do not know what to do next, or you do not know the solution to your problem, then you may resist moving forward with your shadow work. There's a certain comfort in the known, no matter how negative the outcomes may be. Think of it as preferring the devil you know to the one you don't. This attachment to the familiar can be a significant barrier to growth, keeping you tethered to old habits and preventing you from embracing new possibilities.

Breaking through resistance requires practical strategies and a willingness to challenge the status quo, moving beyond the known into the hidden darkness of the unknown. One effective approach is to establish accountability partnerships. Having someone to check in with can provide the motivation needed to push past resistance. This partner could be a friend, a group of like-minded seekers or simply a fellow seeker, or even a therapist—anyone who supports your growth and holds you accountable for your shadow work commitments. Sharing your goals with another person creates a sense of responsibility, making it harder to fall into patterns of avoidance. Additionally, taking incremental steps can make the process feel less overwhelming. Start small, setting achievable goals that gradually lead to more significant changes. This method allows you to build momentum and confidence as you progress, making it easier to sustain your efforts over time.

Consider the story of Crystal, who faced resistance every time she attempted to meditate. She found herself avoiding her practice, feeling unmotivated and stuck. By partnering with a friend who shared similar goals, Crystal introduced a new layer of accountability into her routine. They agreed to text each other each morning, reminding one another to meditate. This simple act of checking in transformed Crystal's approach. She began with just five minutes a day, gradually increasing the time as her resistance waned. Over time, meditation became a natural part of her daily routine and the resistance she once felt dissipated.

Another example is Janet, who struggled with self-sabotage in her journaling practice. Whenever she set a goal to write, she found herself procrastinating, often filling her time with unimportant tasks. Recognizing this pattern, Janet decided to break her journaling into smaller, more manageable segments. Instead of aiming to write for an hour, she committed to just ten minutes a day. This shift made the task feel less daunting, and she began to write more consistently. As she did, she discovered insights into her shadow self that had eluded her before. By "showing up for herself", Janet built trust in herself, creating a foundation for deeper exploration.

These stories illustrate the power of small, consistent actions in overcoming resistance. By recognizing the underlying causes and implementing strategies to counter them, you can move from stagnation to growth. It's a process that requires patience and persistence, but with dedication, you can break free from the constraints of resistance and embrace the full potential of your shadow work.

6.3 NAVIGATING JUDGMENTS FROM SELF AND OTHERS

Judgment can be like a heavy fog, obscuring the path of self-discovery and shadow work. When you set out to explore the hidden aspects of yourself, the judgments you carry—both from within yourself and outside from others—can become significant barriers. Self-criticism is often the most persistent of these, whispering doubts and feeding insecurities. You might hear that voice questioning your worth, calling you an imposter in your own life, or dismissing your efforts as inadequate. This internal dialogue can erode self-acceptance, making it difficult to embrace the shadow aspects that need attention. It's as if you're trying to nurture a garden while constantly pulling at the seedlings, never allowing them to grow. This self-doubt can be compounded by external judgments. When those around you express disbelief or negativity toward your efforts, it reinforces the doubts you already have. You could begin to question your own motives, wondering if the shadow work is worth the effort. The fear of being misunderstood or labeled can stifle your authenticity, tempting you to retreat into a shell of conformity.

To navigate these judgments, you must develop strategies to cultivate self-acceptance and reduce self-criticism. One effective method is through self-compassion exercises. These exercises encourage you to treat yourself with the same kindness and understanding you would offer a dear friend. When that critical voice arises, counter it with affirmations that acknowledge your personal strengths and self-worth. Write down affirmations like "I am enough" or "I accept myself fully" and place them where you can see them daily. Engage in practices that promote self-love, such as journaling about your achievements or meditating on your inherent value as a part of The Expression Of Oneness, God/Goddess. Over time, these practices can shift the internal narrative, allowing you to embrace your shadow with compassion and understanding. This isn't about ignoring your flaws, but understanding they are a part of you that contributes to your humanity.

Facing external fears and judgments requires courage and resilience. It's about maintaining your authenticity even when others don't understand your path. Setting boundaries with critics can help protect your energy and focus. Politely but firmly communicate your needs, expressing that your journey is personal and doesn't require validation from others. This might involve distancing yourself from individuals who consistently undermine your personal growth efforts, or seeking out spaces and places where your exploration is supported. Surround yourself with understanding individuals who respect your process and offer encouragement rather than criticism. These allies can be invaluable, providing a safe haven where you can share your experiences without fear of judgment. They become the voices of support, countering the negative narratives that might otherwise hold you back.

Consider the story of Sarah, a woman who faced judgment from both family and friends when she began her shadow work. Her commitment to self-discovery was met with skepticism, calling it "stupid woo-woo stuff", leaving her feeling isolated and misunderstood. However, Sarah chose to focus on those who supported her journey. She joined a group of like-minded individuals who shared her passion for growth and healing. Within this community, she found validation and encouragement, which helped her maintain authenticity in her shadow work journey, despite external pressures. Sarah's experience highlights the importance of seeking out those who uplift rather than drag you down. By surrounding herself with positive influences, she was able to remain true to herself and continue her shadow work with confidence.

6.4 ADDRESSING THE INNER CRITIC DURING SHADOW WORK

The inner critic is a relentless voice that often emerges during shadow work, casting long shadows over your self-esteem. It whispers doubts, erodes confidence, and chips away at the foundation of self-worth. This internal dialogue is insidious, perpetuating narratives that undermine your sense of self. "I'm not good enough," it says, or "I should be further along by now." These phrases become mantras of self-doubt, echoing through your mind and clouding your perception of reality. The inner critic thrives on comparison, feeding off perceived failures and amplifying them into monumental shortcomings. It sets impossible standards and then chastises you for falling short. But this voice, while loud, is not the truth. It is a distortion, a reflection of past judgments internalized and replayed over time. Understanding its origins can help you begin to dismantle its power and reframe the narrative it spins.

The inner critic often takes root in childhood and past lives, a product of external expectations and societal pressures, or possibly as karma for those pressures you put on others. As children, we learn to navigate the world through the lens of others' perceptions. We absorb their judgments, internalizing them as truths about ourselves. Over time, these external voices morph into our inner critic, carrying forward the weight of past criticisms. This critic becomes a constant companion, lurking in the background and waiting for moments of vulnerability to strike. Possibly, you were overly critical of others in a past life, and now you carry the residual critic in your own head. Recognizing its presence is the first step in silencing its hold. Awareness allows you to identify the specific narratives it perpetuates, shedding light on its pervasive influence on your thoughts and behaviors.

Transforming this inner dialogue into a supportive voice requires intentional effort and practice. One effective strategy is to reframe negative thoughts with positive affirmations. When the critic rears its head, counter its narrative with affirmations that affirm your worth and capabilities. Instead of allowing "I'm not good enough" to linger, replace it with "I am a work in progress, and that's okay." These affirmations serve as reminders of your inherent value, challenging the inner critic's distorted view. Visualization also offers a powerful tool for shifting your internal dialogue. Imagine a nurturing guide, a figure embodying compassion and wisdom, standing beside you. This guide speaks kindly, offering words of encouragement and understanding. Visualizing this supportive presence can help drown out the inner critic's negativity, reinforcing a more positive self-perception.

Real life stories of silencing the inner critic through shadow work abound, offering hope and inspiration. Take, for instance, the story of Sophia, who struggled with feelings of inadequacy in her career. Her inner critic constantly reminded her of past mistakes, undermining her confidence. Through shadow work, Sophia began to confront this critic, using affirmations and visualization to shift her perspective. She envisioned a wise mentor, guiding her with patience and love. Over time, this practice helped Sophia quiet the critic's voice, replacing it with one of self-assurance. She embraced her imperfections as part of her journey on this earth plane, recognizing that growth comes from experience and making mistakes.

Another example is Sheena, who battled an inner critic that mocked her creative pursuits. This voice told her that she lacked talent and that her work would never be good enough. But Sheena refused to let this critic dictate her narrative. She committed to daily affirmations, celebrating her creative expression without judgment. She visualized an audience and clients that valued her art, appreciating it for its uniqueness. Gradually, the critic's voice dimmed, and Sheena found joy in her creations, free from the weight of self-doubt. Her story exemplifies the transformation possible when you face the inner critic head-on, challenging its place in your self-value and reclaiming the power of your own narrative and authenticity.

6.5 SUSTAINING LONG-TERM COMMITMENT TO SHADOW WORK

The path of shadow work is rich and rewarding, yet it demands a steadfast commitment. Consistency is your ally in this transformative process, as meaningful progress hinges on regular practice. Imagine each day as an opportunity to deepen your understanding of yourself, to peel back the layers of your psyche bit by bit. Daily reflection rituals can serve as anchors, keeping you grounded and engaged. Whether it's a few moments of journaling before bed, listening to your favorite songs/mantras/spiritual hymns, or a morning meditation to set the tone for the day, these practices help maintain your connection to the shadow work. They remind you that this exploration is not just a task to be completed but a vital part of your long-term personal growth.

However, like any long-term endeavor, shadow work comes with its own set of challenges. Over time, motivation can wane. The initial excitement of discovery might fade, replaced by routine or even resistance. You might find yourself questioning the value of the work or feeling disheartened by a perceived lack of progress. It can be hard to see the forest for the trees. It's important to remember that these feelings are normal and that every seeker encounters them at some point. The key is to acknowledge them without judgment and find ways to reignite your passion. This might involve revisiting your reasons for starting shadow work in the first place and reminding yourself of the insights and liberation it has already brought.

To keep your practice engaging and fulfilling, setting long-term goals with incremental milestones can be incredibly effective. Break down your overarching objectives into smaller, manageable steps and celebrate each achievement along the way. These milestones serve as markers of progress, reinforcing your commitment and motivation to continue. Perhaps your goal is to cultivate greater self-awareness or to integrate a specific shadow aspect; whatever it may be, recognize and honor each step you take toward it. This approach not only keeps you focused but also helps you appreciate the journey itself, rather than fixating solely on an end result.

Celebrating small victories is another powerful tool in maintaining engagement. Shadow work is a deeply personal and often challenging process, and each breakthrough, no matter how small, deserves recognition. Take a moment to acknowledge your efforts and the courage it takes to confront your shadow. This could be as simple as treating yourself to something, possibly some retail therapy lol, baking some homemade bread, or sharing your success with a trusted friend. These celebrations reinforce the value of your work, reminding you that progress, however gradual, is still progress. They also cultivate a sense of gratitude, helping you stay connected to the positive aspects of your journey.

There are countless stories of individuals who have sustained their commitment to shadow work and experienced profound growth as a result. Consider Lisa, who began her practice with a simple goal: to understand her recurring feelings of inadequacy. She set small, achievable milestones, focusing first on identifying her triggers and then on reframing her self-talk. Over time, these incremental steps led to significant shifts in her self-perception. Each time Lisa reached a milestone, she celebrated by reflecting on how far she'd come, which motivated her to continue. Her dedication paid off, resulting in greater self-compassion and resilience.

Another example is Michelle, who struggled with maintaining her shadow work practice amidst a busy schedule. To stay engaged, she incorporated shadow work into her daily routine, using brief meditation sessions and journaling as a way to check in with herself. She set realistic goals, acknowledging that even a few minutes of reflection each day contributed to her growth. By celebrating the small victories—such as a newfound insight or a moment of clarity—Michelle kept her practice alive and meaningful. Her sustained commitment allowed her to uncover aspects of herself that she'd long ignored, leading to a more authentic and fulfilling life.

As you move forward, remember that a long-term approach is key to unlocking the full potential of shadow work. Embrace the challenges as opportunities for growth, and celebrate each step you take. In doing so, you create a practice that is not only rewarding but also transformative, guiding you toward a deeper understanding of yourself and your shadow. The path is yours to walk, with each day offering new possibilities for self-discovery and integration. With dedication and sincerity, you will find that your shadow holds the key to living a powerfully authentic life.

7
REAL-WORLD APPLICATIONS AND CASE STUDIES

I have heard it said that in the realm of relationships, shadow work can become a beacon of hope, offering a pathway to deeper understanding and connection. Although I have not personally engaged in shadow work in collaboration with a life partner, I do believe that it can be a powerful conduit for growth both on a personal level and together as a couple. I am sure that I tried to get my partner to join me in a shadow work journey, but it wasn't their cup of tea, and I was left to go it alone.

For this reason, we are going to use an imaginary couple, Sarah and Mark, as an example of what can happen when a couple does shadow work together. Sarah and Mark started out as a couple in love and seemed destined for a happy life together, yet found themselves trapped in a cycle of misunderstandings and unresolved conflicts. Their journey through shadow work could reveal not only the complexities of their individual shadows but also the profound transformation that occurs when couples engage in this introspective process together.

Let's pretend that Sarah and Mark's relationship began with an undeniable chemistry. They shared dreams, laughter, and an unspoken bond that seemed unbreakable. However, as time passed, underlying tensions surfaced, leading to frequent arguments and emotional distance. Communication breakdowns became their new norm, with each conversation ending in frustration and tears. Sarah often felt unheard, while Mark struggled with feelings of inadequacy, believing he could never meet Sarah's expectations. These challenges threatened to unravel the love they once cherished, leaving them both feeling isolated and alone.

Through shadow work, Sarah and Mark began to explore the hidden aspects of their personalities that fueled their conflicts. For Sarah, it was a deep-seated fear of abandonment, rooted in childhood experiences of emotional neglect. This fear manifested as a need for constant reassurance, which Mark perceived as criticism. Mark, on the other hand, carried a shadow of self-doubt, stemming from years of comparison to his high-achieving siblings. This led him to interpret Sarah's requests for attention as evidence of his failure. By identifying these shadow aspects, they realized that their arguments were not about each other, but about unresolved wounds from their pasts that colored their interactions.

The process of shadow integration can begin with exercises in active listening, where each partner practices truly hearing the other's perspective without interruption or judgment. This exercise fosters empathy, allowing Sarah to see Mark's vulnerability and Mark to understand Sarah's need for connection. They can also engage in conflict resolution techniques informed by shadow insights, such as identifying triggers and pausing to reflect before responding. These practices help defuse tension and facilitate constructive dialogues. By acknowledging their shadows, Sarah and Mark can learn to approach conflicts with compassion and curiosity, rather than defensiveness.

The transformation potential in their relationship is profound. Trust, which had been eroded by misunderstandings, can begin to be rebuilt. Sarah will feel seen and valued, while Mark will discover a newfound confidence in expressing his feelings. Their emotional connection can deepen, rekindling the love that had drawn them together in the first place. They can then begin to celebrate each other's strengths and support one another's growth, creating a partnership built on mutual respect and understanding. A journey of shadow work together can not only save their relationship but also enrich it, allowing them to thrive individually and as a couple. Sarah and Mark can also begin to express gratitude for the insights they each get through shadow work. Sarah can understand her shadow has empowered her to seek reassurance from within, rather than relying solely on Mark. Mark, meanwhile, can find that confronting his self-doubt enables him to embrace his unique strengths and let go of comparisons. Together, they can realize that their shadows are not obstacles but guides, leading them to a more authentic and fulfilling relationship. This story can serve as an example of the power of shadow work in transforming relationships, offering hope and healing to those willing to explore the depths of their own shadows while within a partnership.

REFLECTION EXERCISE: NAVIGATING YOUR SHADOWS IN RELATIONSHIPS

Consider your own relationships and the dynamics at play. Reflect on the following questions in a journal or during a quiet moment of introspection:

1. What recurring conflicts or misunderstandings arise in your relationships?
2. Can you identify any shadow aspects that might be influencing these interactions?
3. How do past experiences shape your current perceptions and reactions?

4. What steps can you take to integrate these shadow aspects and foster deeper connections?

By engaging with these reflections, you open the door to greater understanding and harmony in your relationships, paving the way for authentic and meaningful connections.

7.1 SHADOW WORK'S IMPACT ON CAREER DEVELOPMENT

In the landscape of professional growth, shadow work plays a critical role in unearthing and addressing the underlying insecurities that often impede career advancement. Many individuals find themselves shackled by self-doubt and the ever-looming specter of imposter syndrome. This feeling of inadequacy can be paralyzing, making even the most competent feel as though they are mere imposters in their work-life roles. For instance, imagine sitting at a meeting, your heart racing as you prepare to speak, convinced that at any moment you will be exposed as a fraud with accusations of inferior intellect or lack of professional experience. This is a common experience for many and highlights the impact of unresolved shadow aspects in the workplace. By engaging in shadow work, individuals come face-to-face with these fears and insecurities, allowing for a more authentic and confident professional presence.

One of the most significant challenges that shadow work addresses is the Resistance To Change, a.k.a. RTC Factor. Many of us have an innate fear of stepping out of our comfort zones, preferring the familiar even when it limits our growth. This reluctance to embrace new opportunities often stems from a shadow aspect that fears failure or the unknown. Through shadow work, we can begin to recognize and untangle these fears, allowing us to welcome change as a catalyst for growth rather than a threat. By acknowledging these shadows, we can develop a mindset that is open to innovation and risk-taking, essential traits for career advancement. There is an old saying, "The only thing consistent in life is inconsistency".

In practical terms, shadow work encourages setting professional boundaries, which is crucial in reducing burnout and maintaining a healthy work-life balance. By understanding and acknowledging the shadow aspects that drive us to overcommit or seek validation through work, we can set limits that protect our well-being. This might involve learning to say no to additional projects or taking time to recharge without guilt. Furthermore, shadow exploration helps us identify our unique strengths, which we can leverage to enhance our career performance. By focusing on these strengths, we can align our work with our true passions and capabilities, leading to greater job satisfaction and success.

Consider the story of Laura, a marketing manager who felt trapped in her role due to pervasive self-doubt and a fear of failure. Through shadow work, Laura uncovered a deep-rooted belief instilled during childhood that she was never good enough. This realization was transformative, allowing her to challenge and reframe these beliefs. As she worked through her shadow, Laura gained the confidence to pursue a leadership role, a position she had long desired but felt unworthy of. By setting boundaries and prioritizing her well-being, Laura found balance in her professional life, leading to increased productivity and fulfillment.

In another instance, shadow work helped Janita, an engineer, address her resistance to change. Janita often felt stuck, unable to pursue new projects despite her talent and potential. Through introspection, she recognized that her fear of stepping into the unknown was rooted in past experiences and haunting past life memories of failure. By confronting this shadow, Janita learned to view change as an opportunity to expand her skill set rather than a threat. This shift in perspective enabled her to take on challenging assignments that showcased her new skills, earning her recognition and advancement within the company. Shadow work empowers us to step into our careers with confidence, authenticity, and a renewed sense of purpose.

7.2 HEALING FROM PAST TRAUMA WITH SHADOW WORK

When it comes to healing from past traumas, shadow work serves as a powerful tool for uncovering and integrating those parts of ourselves that carry the weight of our past. Consider the story of Emily, a woman who faced intense emotional and psychological challenges due to trauma from her childhood and residual anxiety from previous lifetimes of persecution. For years, she rarely went out and became overwhelmed by crowds. She navigated life with an undercurrent of anxiety and fear that seemed inexplicable, always feeling as though something was holding her back. By the age of nineteen, she was suffering from Panic Attacks. Through shadow work, Emily began to identify specific shadows related to her trauma —feelings of unworthiness and deep-seated fear that had rooted themselves in her psyche at a young age.

One therapeutic technique that Emily found particularly helpful was Somatic Experiencing. This practice involves becoming attuned to the body's sensations, allowing the release of trauma that is stored physically. Emily learned to recognize how certain triggers would cause her body to tense up, and through guided exercises, she practiced releasing this tension, thereby reducing the hold her past had on her present. In addition to Somatic Experiencing, narrative-therapy played a key role in reframing her traumatic experiences. By becoming aware of her thoughts and rewriting her internal story, Emily was able to shift the narrative from one of victimhood to empowerment, seeing her past as a source of strength rather than shame.

Emily's healing journey unfolded in stages, each bringing a gradual reduction of panic and trauma symptoms and an increase in resilience. Initially, confronting her shadow was daunting, akin to staring into a mirror and seeing everything that she feared. But with each session, her courage grew, allowing her to delve deeper into the shadows without resistance. As she engaged with her shadow self, Emily noticed a slow but steady transformation. Her anxiety lessened, and she found herself reacting with calm rather than panic in situations that once overwhelmed her. This newfound resilience enabled her to face personal life challenges with a sense of confidence and clarity she had never experienced before.

Reflecting on her healing process, Emily shared that shadow work had granted her a sense of personal strength she didn't know she possessed. She described it as reclaiming parts of herself that had been lost to trauma - having lost pieces of herself, then gathering them back up with compassion and acceptance. Emily realized that her shadows were not enemies but allies in her growth, teaching her lessons about vulnerability, courage, and authenticity. Her experience highlights the profound impact of shadow work in facing parts of our multiple selves that we have locked away and reclaiming them as transporters of personal strength as a catalyst for empowerment and a deeper capacity for healing.

7.3 PRACTICAL APPLICATIONS OF SHADOW WORK IN PARENTING

Parenting is often seen as a mirror reflecting not just the child's growth but also the parent's unresolved shadows. Many of us, whether we realize it or not, project our insecurities and unmet needs onto our children. These projections can arise from our own childhood experiences, echoing patterns that we might not consciously recognize. Imagine a scenario where a parent feels a surge of frustration when their child struggles with schoolwork. This reaction might stem from the parent's own childhood struggles with academic pressure, now unconsciously projected onto their child. By applying shadow work to parenting, we can become more aware of these projections, allowing us to respond with empathy and understanding rather than frustration.

Generational trauma patterns are another area where shadow work can bring healing within families. These patterns often pass down silently, influencing how we parent without us realizing it. Perhaps a mother who experienced emotional neglect as a child finds herself distant with her own children, despite wanting to be more affectionate. Through shadow work, she can identify this pattern, understand its origins, and begin to consciously choose different, more nurturing behaviors. By breaking such cycles, parents can create a more supportive environment for their children, free from the shadows of the past.

Parenting presents a unique set of challenges, often bringing emotional triggers to the surface. For instance, a child's tantrum might trigger a parent's feelings of inadequacy or loss of control. These triggers are opportunities to explore underlying shadow aspects that influence parenting. Balancing discipline with empathy is one such challenge. It requires parents to set personal boundaries while maintaining a compassionate connection with their children. Shadow work helps navigate these waters by encouraging self-reflection and mindfulness, helping to give a parent the space to respond rather than simply react to their children's behavior.

To incorporate shadow work into your parenting approach, consider engaging in reflective journaling about your parenting style and values. Take time to write about your reactions to your child's behavior, exploring any emotions that arise and considering their origins. This practice can illuminate shadow aspects that may be affecting your relationship with your child. Additionally, practicing mindful communication with your children can foster a more connected relationship. This involves listening to your child with full attention, acknowledging their feelings, and expressing your own emotions with clarity and kindness. Such techniques promote mutual understanding and respect, strengthening the parent-child bond.

Consider the story of Maria, a mother who struggled with maintaining patience during her child's meltdowns. Through shadow work, Maria explored her own past, uncovering a childhood filled with strict discipline and little emotional support. By recognizing these shadows, she began to approach her child with increased empathy, seeing tantrums not as a challenge to her authority but as expressions of her child's emotional needs. Over time, Maria's relationship with her child transformed. She was able to step back, gather herself, and be more patient and understanding, fostering safety and trust in their interactions. This shift not only elevated their relationship but also reduced meltdowns and encouraged Maria's child to express emotions more openly, without fear of judgment or being dismissed and punished out of her mother's own frustration.

In another example, Sophia, a working mother of two, found that her stress at work often spilled into home life, leading to impatience with her children. Through shadow work, she identified her underlying fear of failure. Her family had immigrated to America when she was young and the need to succeed was a top priority for her parents. This drive for success fostered her workaholic tendencies. By addressing this shadow, Sophia learned to set healthy boundaries between work and family life. She began to prioritize quality time with her children, using playtime activities to connect with them. This change enriched Sophia's relationship with her children, leading to more joyful interactions, and with the reduced stress, Sophia was able to increase her work productivity while spending less time at work.

These stories illustrate how shadow work can significantly enhance parenting dynamics. By recognizing and integrating our shadows, we can become more attuned to our children's needs, fostering relationships built on love, trust, and mutual understanding. Shadow work empowers us to break free from generational patterns, offering our children a nurturing environment where they can flourish emotionally and spiritually.

7.4 ENHANCING CREATIVITY THROUGH SHADOW INTEGRATION

Creativity is often thought of as a light-filled endeavor, a burst of inspiration that comes from a place of joy. Yet, the shadow holds keys to our creative potential, unlocking doors to new realms of expression. Imagine facing a blank canvas, your heart filled with doubt, the fear of inadequacy whispering that you have nothing new to offer. This is a common block many creatives encounter, where self-criticism silences the muse. However, when we turn to shadow work, we find that these doubts and fears can fuel our creativity. By embracing the shadow, we can break through these barriers, discovering a wellspring of ideas and perspectives that were once hidden away.

One striking example of creativity unlocked through shadow work is the experience of a writer who struggled with persistent writer's block. For years, she felt trapped, unable to translate her thoughts into words. Through shadow work, she explored her fear of vulnerability, rooted in past criticism that left her feeling exposed. By integrating this shadow aspect, she began to write with raw honesty, transforming her vulnerability into a source of power. Her stories, once tentative, now resonated with authenticity and depth, captivating her readers in ways she had never imagined. This transformation illustrates how confronting and integrating our shadows can lead to creative breakthroughs, allowing us to express ourselves more fully and fearlessly.

The relationship between one's shadow and creativity is profound. Our shadows often hold the parts of ourselves we fear or reject, yet these aspects are rich with untapped potential. When we integrate these shadow elements, we open ourselves to innovative thinking and artistic expression. For instance, themes of darkness and conflict that we might avoid in our daily lives can become compelling subjects for creative projects. A painter who once shied away from bold colors and intense emotional themes found liberation in embracing her shadow. By incorporating these elements into her work, she created bold pieces that were not only visually striking but emotionally resonant, capturing the complexity, pain, and confusion of the human experience.

To nurture creativity through shadow integration, consider engaging in creative visualization exercises. These practices involve imagining scenarios where your shadow aspects take center stage, allowing them to inspire new ideas. Picture yourself in a place where your fears and dreams coexist, and let this imagery guide your creative expression. Artistic expression, too, becomes a form of shadow exploration. Whether through painting, writing, or music, you can channel your shadow into your art, creating works that are both personal and universal. This process not only enhances creativity but also fosters self-awareness and healing, as you give voice to the parts of yourself that have long been silent.

Take the story of a musician who grappled with feelings of inadequacy and fear of failure. Shadow work revealed these shadows, rooted in childhood experiences of constant comparison. By acknowledging and integrating these aspects, the musician found the courage to experiment with new sounds and styles. This exploration led to a fresh, unique sound that set her apart, earning her acclaim and satisfaction. Similarly, a visual artist who felt constrained by traditional techniques embraced her shadow's call for freedom. By allowing her intuition to guide her hands, she created abstract pieces that bypassed her logical brain and spoke to her audience in powerful, unexpected ways. Shadow work can elevate creativity to new heights and unlock a treasure trove of inspiration, transforming our fears and doubts into catalysts for artistic self-expression

7.5 FROM POWERLESSNESS TO AUTHENTIC POWER

My own personal shadow journey has led me to uncover and reclaim my authentic power. Although I didn't know it at the time, I was often functioning under a power of "inauthenticity". Meaning, I was acting powerful...but I didn't have any true power behind it. I may have acted big and confident, but I was shaking in my boots. If someone had asked me to define "authentic power", I do not think I would have been able to because it was largely covered up by my own fearful shadows. It almost feels tragic to admit this, and probably why I find the subject of shadow work so compelling. With many years of self-reflection to look back upon, I can now admit that some of the most powerful parts of myself only came to the light of day after many tearful encounters with my own shadow selves. Tears are wonderful, they cleanse and wash away the dirt and grime of previous experiences and memories, allowing for a brighter and clearer vision of ourselves and the world around us. Never fear the tears that come along walking the path of the shadow because they will take you from powerlessness to your authentic power.

In the quiet moments of her life, Emily often felt a deep sense of helplessness. It wasn't that she lacked ambition or talent; rather, she was hemmed in by an invisible barrier that made her second-guess every decision. This sense of powerlessness wasn't just a fleeting feeling; it had woven itself into the fabric of her daily life. From an early age, Emily internalized limiting beliefs—whispers from her past that told her she was never quite good enough. These beliefs were reinforced by societal conditioning, which often dictated who she should be rather than who she was. The weight of these shadows left her feeling trapped, as if her true self was buried beneath layers of expectation and doubt.

The journey to reclaim her power began with acknowledging the shadow aspects that contributed to her sense of inadequacy. Emily recognized that much of her self-doubt stemmed from a childhood where praise was scarce and criticism abundant. These early experiences laid the groundwork for a pervasive fear of failure, a fear that kept her from pursuing her passions and asserting her needs. Emily realized she was not alone in these feelings. Many women carry similar burdens, shaped by cultural norms and familial expectations that prioritize compliance over authenticity. Understanding these shadow aspects was the first step towards dismantling them, allowing her to see them for what they truly were—misguided narratives rather than unchangeable truths of her inherent value.

The transformation process was neither quick nor easy, but it was profoundly liberating. Emily began by practicing self-affirmation, a simple yet powerful tool that helped her rewrite the internal stories she told herself. Each day, she would stand in front of her mirror and declare her worth, affirming her strengths and unique qualities. These affirmations slowly chipped away at the walls of doubt, replacing negativity with self-acceptance. Alongside this, Emily learned to set boundaries, recognizing that saying "no" was not a sign of weakness but an act of self-respect. This newfound skill allowed her to protect her energy and prioritize her well-being, creating space for her true self to flourish.

As she embraced her personal strengths, Emily discovered qualities she had long overlooked. Her empathy, once seen as a vulnerability, became a source of connection and understanding. Her creativity, stifled by fear, blossomed into a vibrant expression of her inner world. By leaning into these strengths, Emily found her voice—a voice that was confident, authentic, and unapologetically her own. She began to take risks she once deemed impossible, pursuing projects that aligned with her passions and values. This shift not only transformed her personal life but also opened doors profession-ally, as she stepped into roles that celebrated her unique perspective.

Reflecting on her journey, Emily described her newfound sense of empowerment as both unexpected and exhilarating. She realized that true power comes from within, rooted in the acceptance of all that she is, shadows and all. The process of embracing her shadow self had unlocked a reservoir of potential she never knew existed. It allowed her to live with a sense of freedom and authenticity she had long yearned for, transforming her life in ways she had never imag-ined. She no longer lived by the precepts of what she "should be doing" or who "she should be", instead she allowed herself to explore her own narratives and her own self-definitions. The very same self-definitions that used to be her source of powerlessness, are now her source of authentic power.

8

EMBRACING WHOLENESS AND TRANSFORMATION

The breeze was gentle, the sun warm, as I stood at the edge of a serene lake, its surface mirroring the sky with uncanny clarity. At that moment, I realized the lake was more than a reflection of the world around it; it was a metaphor for the self. Just as the lake holds the sky and everything above it without judgment or resistance, we too can hold all parts of our selves—our joys, fears, and shadows—with the same gentle acceptance. This was the moment I understood wholeness, not as the absence of flaws, but as the harmonious integration of every aspect of who we are, including the parts we often hide away from or keep hidden from others. Wholeness is the alignment of our conscious and unconscious elements, a symphony where every note, light or dark, plays its part. This is where we bring the sum of all of our selves together, and make our many selves into a whole soul.

Achieving this sense of wholeness requires a journey of self-integration, where the shadow is not shunned but welcomed as a teacher. The first step is a deep reflection on your personal growth and past shadow work experiences. Consider the moments when you confronted a shadow aspect and emerged with a new understanding of yourself. What patterns have you noticed? What lessons have you learned? By reflecting on these pivotal moments, you gain clarity on your journey and the progress you've made. Next, identify the shadow traits that still linger, the ones that subtly influence your actions and thoughts. These might be aspects you've noticed but haven't yet explored deeply.

Once you've identified these shadow traits, the task is to integrate them into your conscious awareness. This means acknowledging their existence, understanding their origins, and embracing them as part of your identity. It involves a dialogue with yourself, where you listen to what these traits have to tell you about your needs, fears, and desires. Integration is not about eradicating these traits, but about finding balance, where your shadow and light coexist in harmony. This process can be challenging, requiring patience and self-compassion. Yet, as you work towards integration, you pave the way for profound psychological benefits.

The psychological, spiritual, and emotional benefits of achieving wholeness are manifold. Increased self-awareness allows you to navigate life with a deeper understanding of your motivations and behaviors, reducing the influence of unconscious patterns - spinning your wheels. Emotional stability emerges as you learn to manage your responses, fostering resilience in the face of life's challenges. With wholeness, you cultivate a sense of peace and acceptance. You are no longer at war with yourself. Instead, you are in tune with your true nature - a beautiful soul that is also a spark of The Infinite Cosmos. This alignment enhances your relationships, as you approach others with empathy and authenticity, understanding that everyone has their shadows to integrate.

Personal stories of integration illuminate the journey to wholeness. Take, for instance, a woman named Clara, who spent years battling self-doubt rooted in a childhood where she was often overshadowed by a more outgoing sibling. Through shadow work, she began to recognize this self-doubt as a shadow aspect, a voice that sought to protect her from vulnerability. By embracing this part of herself and understanding its origins, Clara was able to transform self-doubt into self-assurance, stepping into her own light with confidence and grace. Another story is that of Zoey, who struggled with anger that seemed to erupt unexpectedly. By diving into this shadow, she discovered that her anger was a shield for deep-seated fears of inadequacy. Through shadow integration, she learned to express her emotions constructively, leading to healthier relationships and a newfound sense of peace.

REFLECTION SECTION: EXPLORING YOUR PATH TO WHOLENESS

Take a moment to consider your own journey towards wholeness. What shadow traits have you identified in your life? How have they influenced your actions and relationships? Reflect on a time when you successfully integrated a shadow aspect. How did it change your perspective or behavior? Write down your thoughts and feelings in a journal, allowing yourself to explore these questions with honesty and curiosity. Remember that wholeness is not a destination, but an ongoing process of self-discovery and acceptance. Each step you take brings you closer to living authentically, where every part of you—shadow and light—contributes to the beautiful complexity of your being.

8.1 CELEBRATING THE LIGHT AND DARK WITHIN

One evening, as I was reflecting on the day's events, a thought surfaced—a reminder of how often we shy away from acknowledging the full spectrum of our being. We live in a world that often praises the light while urging us to suppress the dark, but true acceptance means celebrating both. Imagine, for a moment, a magnificent painting that uses only bright colors. Though beautiful, it lacks depth. The shadows, the darker hues, give it dimension and meaning. Similarly, embracing both the light and dark within ourselves is not only liberating but also necessary for a complete and fulfilling life. Holding space for these paradoxes, where our strengths and vulnerabilities coexist, allows us to see the full picture of who we are. This physical earth plane offers an experience of duality.

Balancing opposites is an art, a dance of acknowledging and valuing each side of ourselves without letting one overshadow the other. It's about understanding that our kindness can exist alongside our anger; our confidence with our doubt. This balance is crucial for holistic personal growth. It's not about eradicating darkness, but about integrating it. When we accept that both light and dark are integral to our being, we open up to a richer, more nuanced understanding of ourselves. Our dual nature becomes a source of strength, offering insights and resilience we might otherwise overlook. This acceptance fosters a sense of peace, knowing that we are whole even in our contradictions.

To help you embrace this duality, I suggest a couple of exercises. First, consider journaling prompts that invite you to explore both sides. It's kind of like an exercise in synonyms and antonyms...write about a time when you felt especially strong or capable, and contrast it with a moment of vulnerability. What did each experience teach you? How do they complement each other? This reflection can illuminate how these aspects intertwine, shaping your identity. Another exercise involves visualization. Close your eyes and picture a balance scale, with light on one side and dark on the other. Imagine them harmonizing, each offering its gifts. Visualize the equilibrium, a symbol of your inner harmony. These practices encourage you to honor all parts of your being, celebrating the wholeness that arises from integration.

Stories of transformative acceptance abound, each unique yet universally inspiring. Take, for example, the story of Emily, who always prided herself on being fiercely independent. Yet, beneath this strength lay a shadow of fear—fear of vulnerability and reliance on others. Through shadow work, Emily began to see her independence not as a shield but as one part of a larger picture. She learned to embrace vulnerability, allowing herself to lean on others and deepen her connections. This acceptance transformed her relationships, bringing her peace and authenticity she hadn't known before. Emily also struggled with perfectionism. Her shadow whispered that anything less than perfect was unworthy. By accepting this part of herself, she found freedom in imperfection, discovering creativity and spontaneity she didn't know she possessed.

Celebrating the light and dark within is an ongoing process, a commitment to fearless self-awareness and growth. It invites you to dance with your shadows, to see them not as flaws but as facets of your identity. As you learn to hold space for all parts of your selves, you allow yourself to transmute weakness into power and step into a fuller expression of who you are. This acceptance is transformative, offering a path to peace and empowerment that embraces the beautiful complexity of being human.

8.2 LIVING AUTHENTICALLY WITH YOUR INTEGRATED SELVES

Living authentically is like stepping into a room filled with full colors after being in the shadows of grayscale. It's about aligning who you are inside with how you present yourself to the world. This congruence between your inner and outer selves means embracing not just your strengths, but also those quirks and imperfections you once hid away. Authenticity is freeing because it allows you to live without masks imposed by society, letting your true self shine through. When you live this way, you no longer feel the need to conform to others' expectations or approval. Instead, you find a sense of liberation in being exactly who you are, unfiltered and genuine.

This authenticity can also profoundly impact your personal expression. Imagine speaking your truth without hesitation, expressing your thoughts and feelings with clarity and confidence. The freedom from societal expectations means that you can explore your creativity and self-expression without fear of judgment. Your relationships benefit, too, as authenticity invites real connections. People sense when you're genuine, and it encourages them to be genuine in return, deepening the bonds you share. The energy shifts when you live authentically; it becomes vibrant and alive, reflecting your true essence. This shift enhances not only how you see yourself, but also how you interact with the world around you.

Maintaining this authenticity in daily life requires conscious effort, but it's worth every step. Setting and maintaining personal boundaries is crucial. It involves knowing your limits and behaving in a way where you are sovereign to yourself and communicate them clearly, ensuring that your needs are respected. Boundaries protect your energy and preserve your integrity, allowing you to engage with others from a place of strength. Practicing transparency in communication is another key strategy. This means being open about your thoughts and emotions, even when it's uncomfortable. Honesty fosters trust and understanding, strengthening your relationships and building a supportive community around you. These practices empower you to live authentically, nurturing an environment where you can thrive.

Consider the story of Anna, who spent years conforming to what she thought others expected of her. She realized that she was living a life that wasn't entirely hers. Through shadow work, Anna began to peel back the layers of expectations and connect with her true self. She found that her passion for painting, once sidelined, was a vital part of her identity. By embracing her creativity, Anna not only transformed her career but also forged deeper connections with those around her. Her relationships blossomed as she communicated more openly, sharing her journey with opening to her own self-expression as a painter and inviting others to do the same. Anna's story illustrates the power of authenticity in creating a life filled with meaning and joy.

Then there's Marcia, who always felt a disconnect between her public persona and who she was privately. She often played the role of the perfect professional, even when it didn't align with her values. Through shadow work, Marcia became aware of a past life where she was a male who established a large and thriving empire. But this came at a large personal cost. In that lifetime, he had to disconnect from his emotions and essentially become an Alpha Male Personality, sacrificing the sensitive parts of himself for bold authority. When Marcia integrated this past life shadow of herself, she also developed a deeper purpose in life beyond her job title. She began setting boundaries at work, prioritizing projects that resonated with her true self. This decision led to unexpected opportunities and collaborations, where her creativity and leadership flourished. By integrating her past life shadow self and feeling the emotions that come along with living authentically, Marcia found fulfillment not just in her career but in her personal life, where relationships became more honest and fulfilling. Her journey shows that authenticity isn't just about personal happiness; it can also lead to success and recognition when aligned with your inner truth.

Living authentically is an ongoing practice, a daily commitment to honoring who you are. It requires courage to face and integrate your shadows, but the rewards are profound. As you walk this path, remember that authenticity is not about perfection—it's about being real, embracing all parts of your selves, and sharing that with the world. Your authenticity is your gift, a beacon that invites others to do the same, creating a world where we can all live more fully and fearlessly.

8.3 SHADOW WORK AS A LIFELONG JOURNEY

The essence of shadow work is its ongoing nature. It's not a box to be checked off or a task to be completed. Instead, it's a continuous process that evolves with us, adapting to the changing landscapes of our lives. As we navigate different phases—from youth to maturity, careers to retirement—our shadow aspects shift and transform. What once loomed large in our younger years will soften with age, while new facets emerge, demanding attention. This evolution is a testament to the dynamic nature of our psyche, reminding us that self-discovery is never static. Each phase of life presents its own challenges and opportunities, revealing new layers of our shadow that we have not encountered before.

Consider the transition from early adulthood, where shadows may revolve around identity and belonging, to midlife, where deeper questions of purpose and fulfillment often arise. In each stage, shadow work offers a mirror, reflecting the parts of ourselves that seek integration. This ongoing exploration requires a curious and open mindset, one that embraces the known and unknown. It's about cultivating a sense of wonder about who we are and who we are becoming. It follows us through the stages of Maiden, Mother, and Crone. Journaling or growing a garden can be a faithful companion in this endeavor, providing a space to capture the shifts and insights that emerge over time. Just like how a garden is planted, blooms, and then dies off allowing for new growth, regular reflection allows us to track our own growth, recognize patterns, and honor the journey of becoming more and more of who we truly are.

Legacy is often thought of as the tangible things we leave behind, but it's so much more than that. It's the unseen threads of influence that weave through the lives of those who come after us. Shadow work, with its deep introspection and healing, is a profound way to shape this legacy. By integrating our shadows, we transform not only our selves, but also the dynamics within our families and communities. Our willingness to face and embrace our hidden aspects can ripple through generations, influencing how future family members perceive and interact with their own shadows. When we confront our fears, insecurities, and unhealed wounds, we create an environment where our children and grandchildren feel safe to do the same.

Intentional legacy building through shadow work involves consciously choosing how we want to be remembered and what values we wish to pass on. This process can be as simple as sharing your shadow work practices with your descendants, and teaching them the tools and techniques that have guided you toward healing and self-awareness. Imagine a family where each member is encouraged to explore their inner worlds, where shadow work is as much a part of life as any other spiritual or social tradition. This openness fosters resilience and emotional intelligence, equipping future generations to navigate their own challenges with grace and understanding. Documenting your personal growth journey can also serve as a powerful resource for your family. Journals, letters, scrapbooks, or even video/audio recorded reflections can offer insights into your experiences, becoming a touchstone for those who follow.

The ripple effect of shadow work extends beyond the family to the broader community and society. As individuals transform and integrate their shadows, they become more empathetic, understanding, and connected. These qualities naturally influence interactions with others, fostering a culture of openness and acceptance. Communities, where shadow work is embraced, tend to be more inclusive and supportive, as members feel seen and valued for their whole selves, not just their public personas or what others receive from them. The impact can be profound, creating spaces where diversity is celebrated, and differences are viewed as strengths rather than divisions.

Consider the story of Rachel, who grew up in a family where emotions were rarely discussed. Through shadow work, she broke this cycle, learning to express her feelings and encouraging her children to do the same. Her commitment to emotional transparency has transformed her family's dynamics, creating a legacy of openness and trust. Her children, now adults, carry these values into their own families, continuing the cycle of healing and growth. Another example is Tina, a church and community leader who used shadow work to address her unconscious biases. By acknowledging and integrating these shadows, she fostered a more inclusive environment within her organization, inspiring others to engage in their own shadow exploration. Tina's legacy is one of transformation and empowerment, influencing not just her immediate circle but her community at large.

These stories illustrate that our shadows, when embraced, can be the source of our greatest gifts. They challenge us to grow, to understand ourselves and others, and to leave a legacy that is rich with wisdom and compassion. Shadow work is not just about personal healing; it's a commitment to creating a world where everyone feels empowered to live authentically. In this way, our legacy is not defined by what we have or what others can get from us, but by who we are and the impact we have on those around us. Remember the old saying, "No one cares how much you know until they know how much you care". As we continue this work, we contribute to a legacy of love, understanding, and transformation that echoes far beyond our own lives.

8.4 EMBRACING YOUR TRUE SELF AND THE POWER WITHIN

Embracing your true self through shadow work is a powerful act of reclaiming your personal power and autonomy. It's a process that allows you to stand tall in your own skin, acknowledging every part of yourself—the parts you've celebrated and the ones you've hidden away. This embrace of authenticity is liberating. It means accepting your flaws and strengths alike, and recognizing them as integral to who you are. As you integrate these shadow aspects, you begin to walk with a newfound confidence, and a feeling of being whole and capable. This empowerment isn't about perfection; it's about owning your story, with all its complexities, and stepping into your life with intention and purpose.

This transformation to authenticity doesn't happen overnight. It's a gradual shift, a shedding of the limitations sourced in old layers that no longer serve you and uncovering the inherent power within the truth of your personal story. As you engage in shadow work, you notice the subtle changes in how you perceive yourself and the world. You may find that you're more comfortable in your own company, and less reliant on external validation to feel worthy. The masks you've worn to fit in or please others slowly dissolve, revealing the vibrant truths of who you are. This journey of shadow integration leads to a deeper connection with your inner voice, aligning your actions with your awakened values and desires. It's about living in harmony with yourself, where the choices you make reflect expression of your authentic self.

To help you reflect on this journey and envision what's next, consider engaging in exercises that encourage introspection and visualization. One powerful exercise is to picture your future self, fully embracing your authentic power. Close your eyes and imagine a day in your life five or ten years from now. What does your authentic self look like? How do you spend your time? What relationships nourish you? This visualization can be a guiding star, helping you navigate the choices and challenges that lie ahead. Another exercise involves journaling about your shadow work journey. Reflect on the insights you've gained, the shadows you've integrated, and the aspirations you hold for your future. Writing this book was one of my aspirations. In reality, it has taken me a very long time if you consider the personal growth and maturity it has taken me to get here. I believe that all of us are in the process of " becoming"...becoming more and more of who we really are every day. Even if we don't consciously engage in personal and spiritual growth and development, all of us are in the process "of becoming".

As you continue to embrace your true self, remember that empowerment is a dynamic force. It's not a destination, but a way of living that evolves as you do. Each day offers new opportunities to honor your authenticity, and to make choices that align with your deepest values. By nurturing this empowerment, you create a life that reflects your true essence, one where you can thrive without judgment and inspire others to do the same. Embrace the power of the shadow within you, for it is the source of your greatest potential.

CONCLUSION, BUT NOT THE END OF THE STORY!

As we come to a close of our transformative journey together, I invite you to pause and reflect on the path we've traversed. Throughout this book, we've delved into the depths of the shadow self, using the richness of Hindu goddess archetypes as a guide. We've explored the profound impact of childhood experiences, past lives, and parallel realities on our present existence. By embracing the non-duality of Kali, wisdom of Saraswati, abundance of Lakshmi, and strength of Durga, we've learned to navigate the complexities of our inner landscapes with courage and grace.

Our journey has been one of self-discovery and empowerment. We've learned that the shadow is not a force to be feared or suppressed, but a gateway to wholeness and authenticity. Through practical tools like meditation, journaling, and creative visualization, we've developed the skills to integrate our shadow aspects and cultivate emotional intelligence. We've seen how this work can transform our relationships, careers, and creative pursuits, infusing them with newfound depth and meaning.

As you reflect on your own experiences with shadow work, I encourage you to celebrate the insights and breakthroughs you've achieved. Perhaps you've confronted long-held fears and insecurities or discovered hidden talents and passions. Maybe you've experienced a shift in your relationships, finding greater empathy and understanding. These are the fruits of your dedication and courage, and they are truly worth cherishing and celebrating.

But our journey doesn't end here. Shadow work is a lifelong process, an ongoing commitment to self-discovery and growth. As you continue on this path, I invite you to make shadow work a regular practice in your life. Set aside time each week and later each month for introspection and self-reflection. Engage with the exercises and prompts in this book whenever you feel called to do so. Seek out communities of like-minded individuals who share your passion for personal development. By staying engaged with your shadow, you'll continue to peel back the layers of your being, revealing ever-greater depths of wisdom and self-understanding.

As you integrate the lessons of this book into your daily life, I encourage you to approach each moment with curiosity and compassion. Remember that every challenge, every trigger, every emotional upheaval, every tear, is an opportunity for growth and transformation. By meeting these experiences with an open heart and a willingness to learn, you'll develop resilience and adaptability in the face of life's ups and downs.

Ultimately, the goal of shadow work is not just personal transformation, but collective healing. As you embrace your own shadow and step into your authentic power, you become a beacon of light for others. Your courage and vulnerability inspire those around you to embark on their own journeys of self-discovery. By sharing your experiences and insights with others, you contribute to a global awakening, a shift towards greater compassion, understanding, and unity.

As we conclude our time together, I want to express my deepest gratitude for your openness, bravery, and your commitment to growth. It has been an honor to share my stories and guide you through this transformative process, and I am confident that the seeds we've planted together will continue to blossom in your life. Remember, you are not alone on this journey. The wisdom of the goddesses, the support of your community, and the strength of your own spirit are always with you.

So go forth, dear seeker, and embrace the fullness of who you are. Dance with your shadows, celebrate your light, and know that you have the power to create a life of profound beauty and authenticity. The path may not always be easy, but it is always worth taking. Trust in the journey, trust in yourself, and know that the universe is always conspiring in your favor.

With love and gratitude,

Leah

For more information about Leah or HealHouz please visit https://healhouz.com/ or email support@healhouz.com

MAKE A DIFFERENCE WITH YOUR REVIEW

Now that you have more tools and treasures in your Shadow Work tool chest, I would like to ask you to please pass on your new found knowledge to other Shadow Work self-help seekers and let them know where they can find the same tools and treasures.

- You can do so, by leaving your honest opinion and review on the platform where you purchased your book. Navigate to the book's product page on the online retailer (like Amazon, Barnes & Noble, Kobo, Google Play, Apple/Kindle Book App).
- Log into your account or product page, and locate the "Write a Review" section to share your thoughts and rating about the book; make sure you're logged in with the account that made the purchase to leave a verified review.
- Or you can leave a book review at https://healhouz.com/

Thank you again for your personal contribution to transformation through Shadow Work.

REFERENCES

- *Ancient Greek and Hindu Goddesses as Archetypes of our …* https://www.joannakujawa.com/ancient-greek-and-hindu-goddesses-as-archetypes-of-our-lives/
- *Inner Childhood Wounds: Healing Using Shadow Work* https://rediscoveringsacredness.com/inner-childhood-wounds-healing-using-shadow-work/
- *What Past-Life Regression Therapy Can Do For You* https://aspacebetween.com.sg/articles/therapy-approaches/grow-beyond-your-past-what-past-life-regression-therapy-can-do-for-you
- *The Akashic Records and the Holographic Universe* https://www.hinduamerican.org/blog/the-akashic-records-and-the-holographic-universe/
- *What Goddess Kali teaches us about Shadow Work.* https://www.elephantjournal.com/2021/12/shadow-lessons-from-the-goddess-kali/#:~:text=When%20we%20commit%20to%20shadow,are%20both%20creators%20and%20destroyers.
&text=If%20what%20we%20want%20to,blessing%2C%20dancing%2C%20and%20mothering.
- *(PDF) A Literature Review on Vipassana Meditation* https://www.researchgate.net/publication/383260999_A_Literature_Review_on_Vipassana_Meditation_Psychological_Treatment_and_Social_Benefits_for_Harmonizing_the_Inner_Self_and_Society
- *Healing With Shadow Work Meditation* https://insighttimer.com/blog/hidden-self-shadow-work-meditation/
- *100+ Deep Shadow Work Prompts To Accept Yourself And …* https://www.scienceofpeople.com/shadow-work-prompts/
- *What Goddess Kali teaches us about Shadow Work.* https://www.elephantjournal.com/2021/12/shadow-lessons-from-the-goddess-kali/
- *12 Time Management Skills in Spiritual Life* https://amitray.com/12-time-management-skills/
- *How to Create Space for Introspection* https://sunriseranch.org/how-to-create-space-for-introspection/
- *Jungian Therapy: Definition, Techniques, and Efficacy* https://www.verywellmind.com/what-is-jungian-therapy-5211138

- *Projection: The Great Threat to Intimate Relationships* https://www.psychologytoday.com/us/blog/evolution-the-self/202103/projection-the-great-threat-intimate-relationships
- *How to Identify, Heal, & Integrate Your Emotional Triggers* https://rediscoveringsacredness.com/how-to-identify-heal-integrate-your-emotional-triggers/
- *Roar Like a Goddess: Becoming Unapologetically ...* https://selineshenoy.com/thedreamcatcherpodcast/roar-like-a-goddess
- *Understanding Shadow Work: Overview, Exercises & ...* https://damorementalhealth.com/understanding-shadow-work/
- *Inner Child Work: 15+ Practical Tools* https://positivepsychology.com/inner-child-healing/
- *Goddess Kali and the Practice of Non Duality* https://www.movingarchetypes.com.au/blog/goddess-kali#:~:text=In%20Indian%20spirituality%2C%20Goddess%20Kali,of%20the%20Goddess%20Kali%20practice.
- *A Ritual to Honor the Goddess Lakshmi* https://orderwhitemoon.org/goddess/lakshmi-devi/lakshmi-ritual.html
- *Meditation And Mantra For Saraswati Devi | Rachel Zinman* https://insighttimer.com/rachelzinman/guided-meditations/meditation-and-mantra-for-saraswati-devi
- *How to Release Fear in 4 Steps | Healing & Shadow Work* https://www.adventuringwithposeidon.com/blog/how-to-release-fear-in-4-steps#:~:text=The%20only%20way%20to%20release,into%20fight%2C%20flight%20or%20freeze.
- *Tantra & Kali: Understanding the Goddess Archetype* https://beneaththelayers.com/2022/10/06/tantra-kali-understanding-the-goddess-archetype/
- *Feeling overwhelmed? Try these 6 emotional resilience tips* https://www.calm.com/blog/feeling-overwhelmed
- *Living With the Inner Critic: 8 Helpful Worksheets (+ PDF)* https://positivepsychology.com/inner-critic-worksheets/
- *Carrying the Unconscious of Others: Shadow Work in ...* https://www.leylaaylin.com/post/carrying-the-unconscious-of-others-shadow-work-in-relationship
- *The Essential Guide to Shadow Work* https://www.conni.me/blog/shadow-work
- *Inner Childhood Wounds: Healing Using Shadow Work* https://rediscoveringsacredness.com/inner-childhood-wounds-healing-using-shadow-work/#:~:text=Shadow%20work%20is%20a%20powerful,into%20personal%20growth%20and%20healing.

- *Shakti, Lakshmi, Parvati, Saraswati, Durga, Kali | Intro to ...* https://library.fiveable.me/introduction-hinduism/unit-4/major-hindu-goddesses-shakti-lakshmi-parvati-saraswati-durga-kali/study-guide/8yPxyRhgvz1QuwdR
- *The Burning Times* https://en.wikipedia.org/wiki/The_Burning_Times
- *Let Them Theory: Mel Robbins' new book.* (n.d.). https://www.melrobbins.com/letthemtheory
- *Dr. Ibrahim Karim.* (n.d.). Biogeometry-2015. https://www.biogeometry.ca/dr-ibrahim-karim
- Wikipedia contributors. (2024, December 22). *The Burning Times.* Wikipedia. https://en.wikipedia.org/wiki/The_Burning_Times
- *The official website of Dr Joe Dispenza.* (n.d.). https://drjoedispenza.com/
- *Dolores Cannon.* (2024, April 3). Dolores Cannon. https://dolorescannon.com/
- Wikipedia contributors. (2024, May 17). *José Argüelles.* Wikipedia. https://en.wikipedia.org/wiki/Jos%C3%A9_Arg%C3%BCelles
- Wikipedia contributors. (2025, February 9). *Dorothy Eady.* Wikipedia. https://en.wikipedia.org/wiki/Dorothy_Eady
- Admin. (2024, September 10). *Abraham-Hicks Publications - Law of Attraction Official site.* Home of Abraham-Hicks Law of Attraction. https://www.abraham-hicks.com/
- *Shadow Work Dark Goddess Magic* https://www.moderngoddessliving.com/goddess-blog/shadow-work-embracing-your-darkest-self-to-find-personal-alchemy-and-healing
- *GALACTIC CENTER BY JONI PATRY.* (n.d.). GALACTIC CENTER BY JONI PATRY. https://www.galacticcenter.org/
- Ina. (2024, November 18). Just let them - ina - medium. *Medium.* https://medium.com/@ukative/just-let-them-b14e41eac141
- *Kali: Goddess of Destruction as a Guide for Transformation* https://selenamadden.wordpress.com/2016/01/23/kali-goddess-of-destruction-as-a-guide-for-transformation/
- Scott, E., PhD. (2024, February 12). *What is body scan meditation?* Verywell Mind. https://www.verywellmind.com/body-scan-meditation-why-and-how-3144782
- *The Importance of Awareness, Acceptance, and Alignment ...* https://pmc.ncbi.nlm.nih.gov/articles/PMC8895697/
- *Dancing with Shadow; a key to unlocking great leadership* https://www.linkedin.com/pulse/dancing-shadow-key-unlocking-great-leadership-nicole-barrett

Made in the USA
Columbia, SC
27 July 2025

f60fe9b7-341b-4ef0-9eae-8c780128c83fR01